AMERICAN INDIANS
OF CALIFORNIA, THE GREAT BASIN, AND THE SOUTHWEST

NATIVE AMERICAN TRIBES

AMERICAN INDIANS OF CALIFORNIA, THE GREAT BASIN, AND THE SOUTHWEST

EDITED BY KATHLEEN KUIPER, MANAGER, ARTS AND CULTURE

Britannica
Educational Publishing

IN ASSOCIATION WITH

ROSEN
EDUCATIONAL SERVICES

Published in 2012 by Britannica Educational Publishing
(a trademark of Encyclopædia Britannica, Inc.)
in association with Rosen Educational Services, LLC
29 East 21st Street, New York, NY 10010.

First Edition

Britannica Educational Publishing
Michael I. Levy: Executive Editor
J.E. Luebering: Senior Manager
Adam Augustyn: Assistant Manager, Encyclopædia Britannica
Marilyn L. Barton: Senior Coordinator, Production Control
Steven Bosco: Director, Editorial Technologies
Lisa S. Braucher: Senior Producer and Data Editor
Yvette Charboneau: Senior Copy Editor
Kathy Nakamura: Manager, Media Acquisition
Kathleen Kuiper: Manager, Arts and Culture

Rosen Educational Services
Jeanne Nagle: Senior Editor
Nelson Sá: Art Director
Cindy Reiman: Photography Manager
Karen Huang: Photo Researcher
Brian Garvey: Designer, Cover Design
Introduction by Kathleen Kuiper

Library of Congress Cataloging-in-Publication Data

American Indians of California, the Great Basin, and the Southwest/edited by Kathleen Kuiper.
    p. cm.—(Native American tribes)
"In association with Britannica Educational Publishing, Rosen Educational Services."
Includes bibliographical references and index.
ISBN 978-1-61530-682-4 (library binding)
1. Indians of North America—West (U.S.)—History. 2. Indians of North America—West
(U.S.)—Social life and customs. I. Kuiper, Kathleen.
E78.W5A57 2012
978.004'97—dc23

                                                                        2011028073

Manufactured in the United States of America

On the cover: Shoshone woman in traditional dress sits outside of a buckskin tepee.
Marilyn Angel Wynn/Nativestock/Getty Images

On page viii: Hopi Kachina and rug. *Lynn Johnson/National Geographic Image Collection/
Getty Images*

On pages 1, 19, 42, 60, 74, 93, 119, 120, 122, 127: A Pomo feather basket. *Shutterstock.com*

CONTENTS

Introduction   viii

Chapter 1: California Indians   1
  Cultural Characteristics   3
    Territorial and Political
    Organization   3
    Local Organization   4
    Ownership and Trade   5
    Authority   6
    Subsistence and Economic
    Strategies   7
    Religious Beliefs and Practices 8
    Soul Loss   11
    Marriage and Family   12
    Oral Tradition and the Arts   13
  Missions, Colonization,
  and Change   14
    Junípero Serra   15

**Chapter 2: California Peoples
in Focus**   19
  Cahuilla   19
    Katherine Siva Saubel   20
  Chumash   21
  Costanoans   22
  Diegueños   23
    Mission Indians   24
  Gabrielino   25
  Hupa   26
  Luiseño   28
  Maidu   29
  Miwok   30
  Mono   31
  Pomo   32

Serrano	33
Shasta	34
Wintun	35
Yana	36
Yuki	37
Yurok	39

Chapter 3: Great Basin Indians   **42**
Cultural Characteristics	43
Language	44
Hokan Languages	44
Transportation, Shelter, Tools, and Subsistence	45
Social Conditions	50
Kinship, Marriage, and Family	51
Religious Beliefs and Practices	52
Vision Quest	54
First Contact and After	55

Chapter 4: Great Basin Peoples in Focus   **60**
Comanche	60
Quanah Parker	63
Mono	65
Northern Paiute	66
Sarah Winnemucca	67
Shoshone	68
Sacagawea	70
Southern Paiute	72
Washoe	73

Chapter 5: Southwest Indians   **74**
Cultural Characteristics	75
Language	76
Food Production and Social Structure	78
Pueblo Architecture	79

Family and Education   80
Kachinas   82
Religious Beliefs and Practices   83
Blessingway   85
Colonization and Change   86
Resistance to Colonization   86
Methods of Cultural
Preservation   88
Developments in the 20th and
21st Centuries   90

**Chapter 6: Southwest Peoples
in Focus**   **93**
Yumans, Pima, and Tohono
O'odham   93
Yumans (Hokan Speakers)   95
Pima and Tohono O'odham
(Uto-Aztecan Speakers)   97
Pueblo Indians   100
Hopi (Uto-Aztecan)   106
Zuni (Penutian)   108
Apacheans (Athabaskan
Speakers)   109
Apache   112
Cochise   115
Navajo   116

Conclusion   119

Glossary   120
Bibliography   122
Index   127

INTRODUCTION

Children's toys are among the world's best teaching tools simply because they flip on the switch of the imagination. Take, for instance, the kachina dolls that Pueblo Indian girls are given. Although they become deeply familiar to those who play with them, these figures hold a continuing fascination that lifts them above the realm of the everyday. Kachina dolls represent the all-important kachina spirits of the Pueblo religion. They are talismans, of sorts, that embody the group's origin myths and life ways. The more the dolls are held and examined as stories are told, the more their mystery and power are enhanced. Familiarity with their heft and appearance makes them linger in the mind. Memorization of the kachina's characteristic gestures, tools, dress, and behaviour is part of a child's cultural integration.

Religious beliefs and practices, as symbolized by Pueblo kachina dolls, are only one of the elements that define a culture. Others include food and how it is obtained; domesticated animals, modes of transportation, tools, social organization, and language; how clothing and vessels are made; decorative and fine arts, and so on. The peoples who share similar ways of life make up what anthropologists call a culture area. This book delves deeply into three culture areas of the so-called New World: California, Great Basin, and Southwest Indians.

Of the three groups mentioned, the California Indians were the most abundant. The region's great variety of microenvironments provided a plentiful supply of foods and materials. The indigenous peoples of California were considerably more politically stable, sedentary, and conservative, and less in conflict with one another than was generally the case in other parts of North America. Within the California culture area, neighbouring groups often had elaborate systems for the exchange of goods and services. In general, the California tribes reached levels of cultural and material complexity rarely seen among hunting-and-gathering cultures.

In addition to their prosperity, the California Indians differed from the Eastern tribes in their main non-native adversaries. Rather than European settlers in search of land and freedom from tyranny overseas, the California peoples faced Spanish missionaries in search of converts and tribute.

The process of missionization began in Mexico, under the direction of the Spanish Franciscan priest Junípero Serra. After working among the Mexican Indians, first in Sierra Gorda and then in south-central Mexico, Serra joined the Spanish military officer Gaspar de Portolá in an attempt to secure Spanish claims to what is now the state of California. Their expedition to the north began in 1769. In that same year, Serra founded a mission in San Diego, the first of 21 stations that would stretch up the California coast. Spanish missionary efforts came to an end in the early 19th century, and their record was one of distinctly mixed success. The missionaries in North America never received the full support of the Spanish government, as had their counterparts in the south, which was the heart of the Spanish American empire. Further, they failed to learn the languages of the Native American population, which made communication difficult at best and true conversion virtually impossible.

When the missions were finally secularized in 1833, some 30,000 Mission Indians were farming under the direction of priests and soldiers at the various missions. Disease had ravaged the indigenous population for decades after the Spaniards' arrival. During the remainder of the 19th century, thousands of indigenous Californians were enslaved through the application of antivagrancy laws. Thousands of others were killed during state-sponsored raids that were touted as "pacification" efforts. By 1880 only about 15,000 California Indians remained, a reduction of about nine-tenths of their pre-Columbian population level.

During the 20th century, as the California Indian population began to recover, Native American communities promoted a variety of advocacy and cultural-renewal activities. During World War II California's burgeoning military-industrial complex drew people from across the country. Following the war, the state became a destination point for U.S. Bureau of Indian Affairs relocation programs. These factors caused many Native Americans from other parts of the United States to relocate to the state. By the early 21st century, California had the largest Native American population in the United States, the vast majority of which resided in urban areas.

The relatively dense population of early California Indians stood in stark contrast to the sparse population of the Great Basin. Composed of most of the present-day states of Utah and Nevada; large parts of Oregon, Idaho, Wyoming, and Colorado; and smaller parts of Arizona, Montana, and California, the Great Basin was characterized by arid to semiarid conditions that made food relatively scarce. This condition applied until the introduction of the horse, which brought about the greatest changes to the American West.

Horses were introduced to the Americas in the 1500s by the Spanish conquistadores. Other than guns and the germs to which the indigenous peoples had no immunity, horses provided the biggest advantage to the conquerors in their march northward. Not surprisingly, the response to the horse has proven to be the usual defining feature of the Great Basin peoples. Those of the north and east—the Southern Utes and the Eastern Shoshone—were the first Indians of the Great Basin to adopt a horse-based culture. As they and others did so, they began to share the features of the Plains Indians that the use of the horse made possible, including the wholesale hunting of bison (buffalo) and intertribal trade and warfare.

The Comanche—who originated in the Great Basin but ultimately swept through the Plains, scattering less aggressive tribes in their wake—were the most successful adaptors of the horse. They became master breeders, producing fast ponies with great endurance. This enabled them to keep pace with buffalo herds and lance them on the run, thus avoiding the charge of the wounded animal.

Perhaps more significantly, the Comanche mastered the art of horse warfare. Their young men practiced riding tricks such as dropping their bodies to the horse's side in order to screen them from the enemy and learned to shoot arrows rapidly at a gallop. In the earliest years of combat with Native American groups, frontiersmen had to dismount to aim, shoot, and reload their rifles. Not until the invention and dissemination of the Colt six-shooter did settlers stand a chance against the Comanche and their friends.

The Great Basin Indians that remained pedestrian and did not adopt horses diverged greatly from the horse cultures. They traveled with domesticated dogs pulling their travois from one seasonal camp to another. Their diet consisted chiefly of seed and root plants, supplemented by fish and small game such as rabbits and water birds.

One outstanding feature of the Great Basin groups was the prominence of shamans, individuals believed to achieve various powers through trance or ecstatic religious experience. Shamans were typically thought to have the ability to heal the sick, communicate with the otherworld, and escort the souls of the dead to the otherworld. Peoples of the Great Basin shared this religious system with a number of groups of northern Asia, including the Khanty, Mansi, Tungus, Chukchi, and Koryak. This is noteworthy because the populating of the Americas is believed to have occurred at least in part by means of migration across the Bering Land Bridge (Beringia) between northeastern Asia and northwestern North America.

Shamans, who could be of either sex, were usually distinguishable from the rest of the group by certain mental and physical characteristics. These might include a sensitive, mercurial, or eccentric personality and/or such physical defects as lameness or an extra finger or toe. Such exceptional traits were thought to be an indication of chosen-ness. The spirit-being—and sometimes other beings as well—became the shaman's guide. It instructed him or her how to cure diseases, foretell the future, and practice sorcery. Sometimes shamans also apprenticed with an older, practicing mentor from whom they learned rituals and cures.

Like the Great Basin, the Southwest culture area is characterized by an arid environment. Believed to be pervaded by kachina spirits, this region contains austere and picturesque cliff dwellings built and then abandoned by the Ancient Pueblo (Anasazi) culture (c. 100 to 1600 CE). Modern Pueblo tribes, including the Hopi, Zuni, Acoma, and Laguna, are descended from the Ancestral Puebloans, whose culture was centred generally on the area where the boundaries of what are now the U.S. states of Arizona, New Mexico, Colorado, and Utah intersect. Natives in the earlier of the so-called Basketmaker periods (100-500 BCE) had an economy characterized by hunting, gathering wild plant foods, and some maize (corn) cultivation. These people typically lived in caves or in shallow pit houses constructed in the open. They also made pits in the ground that they used to store food. Their habitation sites contained many examples of fine basketry.

The later Basketmaker period (500-750 BCE) was marked by the increasing importance of agriculture, including the introduction of bean crops and the domestication of turkeys. To support their agricultural pursuits and increasing population, the people built irrigation structures such as reservoirs and check dams (low stone walls used to slow the flow of rivulets and streams), thereby increasing soil moisture and decreasing erosion. Hunting and gathering continued, although in supplementary roles. An increasingly sedentary way of life coincided with the widespread use of pottery. These people resided in relatively deep semisubterranean houses that were located in caves or on mesa tops.

During the first Pueblo period (750-950) most building shifted above ground, and a number of very large communities were built, some with more than 100 adjoining rooms. Stone masonry began to be used, and kivas (the underground circular chambers used henceforth primarily for ceremonial purposes) became important community features. Cotton was introduced as an agricultural product; pottery assumed a greater variety of shapes, finishes, and decorations; and basketry became less common. Throughout this period, the area of Ancestral Pueblo occupation continued to expand, and new communities began to be built in canyons, in addition to the traditional mesa-top locations.

The third Pueblo period (1150-1300) was the era of the spectacular cliff dwellings. These villages were built in sheltered recesses in the faces of cliffs but otherwise differed little from the masonry or adobe houses and villages built previously. Large, freestanding apartment-like structures were also built along canyons or mesa walls. In all of these settings, dwellings often consisted of two, three, or even four stories, generally built in stepped-back fashion so that the roofs of the lower rooms served as terraces for the rooms above. (This characteristic style can also be seen in contemporary pueblos.) These structures had anywhere from 20 to as many as 1,000 rooms. The population became concentrated in these large communities, and many smaller villages and hamlets were abandoned. Agriculture continued to be the main economic activity, and craftsmanship in pottery and weaving achieved its finest quality during this period.

Ancestral Pueblo people abandoned their communities by about 1300 CE as a result of a convergence of cultural and environmental factors. The Great Drought (1276–99) probably caused massive crop failure, and rainfall continued to be sparse and unpredictable until approximately 1450. At the same time, and perhaps in relation to the Great Drought's impact on the availability of wild foods, conflicts increased between the Ancestral Pueblo and ancestral Navajo and Apache groups. During the period lasting from 1300 to 1600, the Ancestral Pueblo moved to the south and the east, building new communities in places where gravity-based irrigation works could be built, including the White Mountains of what is now Arizona and the Rio Grande valley.

The history of the modern Pueblo tribes is usually dated from approximately 1598 onward, when Spanish colonial occupation of the North American Southwest began. In their attempt to Christianize and exact tribute for the crown from the indigenous peoples of the Southwest, the Spanish often used violence. The hostility this engendered in the Pueblo culminated in a successful regional revolt in 1680. Pueblo tribes remained free of Spanish authority for 14 years. By the early 18th century, epidemic disease and colonial violence had reduced the indigenous population and the number of Pueblo settlements, which had fallen from approximately 75 to between 25 and 30 communities. Despite these changes, many aspects of Ancestral Pueblo culture—including languages, agricultural practices, and craft production—persist among the contemporary Pueblo peoples of the Southwest.

Closely examining the various features predominant within the California, Great Basin, and Southwest culture areas leads to a greater understanding of these groups of native peoples. Ideally, such study also should spark further conversation about broader issues of settlement, conquest, and cultures in conflict.

Chapter 1
CALIFORNIA INDIANS

The Native American peoples who have traditionally resided in the area roughly corresponding to the present states of California (U.S.) and northern Baja California (Mex.) are known as California Indians.

The peoples living in the California culture area at the time of first European contact in the 16th century were only generally circumscribed by the present state boundaries. Some were culturally intimate with peoples from neighbouring areas. For instance, California groups living in the Colorado River Valley, such as the Mojave and Quechan (Yuma), shared traditions with the Southwest Indians, while those of the Sierra Nevada, such as the Washoe, shared traditions with the Great Basin Indians, and many northern California groups shared traditions with the Northwest Coast Indians.

A mosaic of microenvironments—including seacoasts, tidewaters, rivers, lakes, redwood forests, valleys, deserts, and mountains—provided ample sustenance for its many residents and made California one of the most densely populated culture areas of Northern America. The indigenous peoples of this region were considerably more politically stable, sedentary, and conservative and less in conflict with one another than was generally the case in other parts of North America. Within the culture area neighbouring groups often developed elaborate systems for the exchange of goods and services. In general, the California tribes reached levels of cultural and material complexity rarely seen among hunting and gathering cultures.

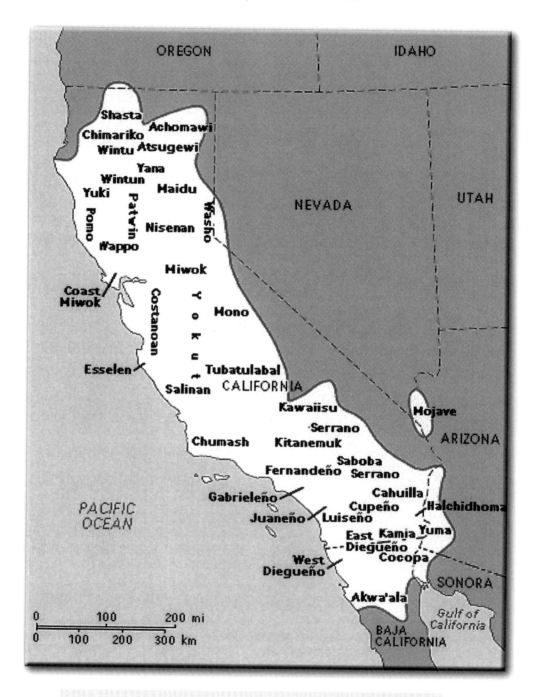

Distribution of California Indians. Encyclopædia Britannica, Inc.

CULTURAL CHARACTERISTICS

A study of several characteristics helps reveal the nature of life among the California Indians. These traits include their social organization, their typical settlement patterns, the items within their material culture and the manner in which these items are produced, notions of property, attitudes regarding marriage and family, religious practices, arts, and so on.

TERRITORIAL AND POLITICAL ORGANIZATION

A large and diverse grouping of tribes—each with its own language, belief system, and traditions—inhabited the California culture area. California peoples for the most part avoided centralized governmental structures at the tribal level, preferring instead to operate as many independent geopolitical units, or tribelets. These were tightly organized polities that nonetheless recognized cultural connections to the other polities within the tribe. They were perhaps most analogous to the many independent bands of Sioux. Tribelets generally ranged in size from about a hundred to a few thousand people, depending on the richness of locally available resources. Tribelet territories ranged in size from about 50 to 1,000 square miles (130 to 2,600 square km).

Within some tribelets all the people lived in one principal village, from which some of them ranged for short periods of time to collect food, hunt, or visit other tribelets for ritual or economic purposes. In other tribelets there was a principal village to which people living in smaller settlements traveled for ritual, social, economic, and political occasions. A third variation involved two or more large villages, each with various satellite settlements. In such systems, a designated "capital" village would be the residence of the principal chief as well as the setting for major rituals and political and economic negotiations.

LOCAL ORGANIZATION

Tribelets throughout most of California typically established permanent villages that they occupied year-round, although small groups routinely left for short or more extended periods (a few days to a few weeks) to hunt or forage. Much depended on supplies immediately available. In areas with sparse economic resources, seminomadic bands of 20 to 30 individuals were common, though these would gather seasonally in larger groups for such activities as antelope drives and piñon-nut harvests. As a rule, riverine and coastal peoples enjoyed a more settled life than those living in the desert and foothills.

Traditional house types varied from permanent, carefully constructed homes occupied for generations to the most temporary types of structures. Dwellings could be wood-framed (northern California), earth-covered (various areas), semisubterranean (Sacramento area), or made of brush (desert areas) or thatched palm (southern California). Communal and ceremonial buildings were found throughout the region and were often large enough to hold the several hundred people who could be expected to attend rituals or festivals. Houses ranged in size from 5 or 6 feet (almost 2 metres) in diameter to apartment-style buildings in which several families lived together in adjoining units. Sweat lodges were also common. These earth-covered permanent structures were used by most California tribes (the Colorado River groups and the northern Paiute, on the margins of California, were exceptions), with sweating a daily activity for most men.

The Chumash lived in homes made by covering a sapling frame with brush. Marilyn Angel Wynn/Nativestock.com/Collection Mix: Subjects/ Getty Images

OWNERSHIP AND TRADE

In native California, concepts of property ownership typically varied by degree rather than by nature. Land was generally owned by larger groups such as clans and villages, which protected it from incursions by other groups. Instead of owning land, individuals, lineages, and extended families exercised exclusive use rights (usufruct) to certain food-collecting, fishing, and hunting areas within the communal territory. Areas where resources such as medicinal plants or obsidian (a form of volcanic glass used to make very sharp tools) were unevenly distributed over the landscape might be owned by either groups or individuals. Particular articles could be acquired by manufacture, inheritance, purchase, or gift.

Goods and foodstuffs were distributed through recip-
rocal exchange between kin and through large trading
fairs, which were often ritualized. Both operated similarly
in that they served as a redistribution and banking system
for easily spoiled food; a group with surplus edibles would
exchange them for durable goods (such as shells) that
could be used in the future to acquire fresh food in return.

Most California groups included professional traders
who traveled long distances among the many tribes; goods
from as far away as Arizona and New Mexico could be
found among California's coastal peoples. Generally, shells
from the coastal areas were valued and exchanged for
products of the inland areas, such as obsidian. Medicines,
manufactured goods such as baskets, and other objects
were also common items of exchange.

AUTHORITY

The chief or leader of organized groups or tribelets usually achieved the position through heredity. Chiefs were
mostly men, although in some groups, such as the Pomo,
women were eligible for the office. Administrative matters, particularly as they pertained to the economic welfare
of the group, were left to the chief. Duties ranged from
matter-of-course admonitions to specific directions for
particular tasks, such as indicating where food was available and how many people would be required to collect it.
Such leaders redistributed the economic resources of the
community and, through donations from its members,
maintained resources from which emergency needs could
be met. In some areas the chief also functioned as a priest,
maintaining the ceremonial house and ritual objects.

Within their communities, chiefs were the major
decision makers and the final authority, although they
typically worked with the aid of a council of elders, heads

of extended families, ritualists, assistant chiefs, and shamans. The chief was generally a conspicuous person, being wealthier than the average individual, more elaborately dressed, and often displaying symbols of office. Chiefs' families formed a superstratum of the community elites, especially among those tribelets that organized themselves through lineages.

As chiefs led in the political sphere of traditional native California life, shamans led in the sphere in which spiritual and physical health intertwined. The vocation of shaman was open to women and men. Shamans enjoyed a status somewhat similar to that of chief. They served as physical and mental healers, diviners, advisers, artists, and poets. Among other duties, they defined and described the world of the sacred and regulated the fortune of souls before and after death, mediating between the mundane and sacred worlds. Most tribelets in California had one or more shamans, who were active in political life, working with other leaders and placing their powers at the disposal of the community.

Alongside chiefs and shamans were ritualists—dancers, singers, fire tenders, and others—who were carefully trained in their crafts and who functioned intimately within the political, economic, and religious spheres of their communities. These men and women acquired considerable respect and often wealth because of their skills. In effect, they were members of the power elite. When performing, ritualists were usually costumed in headdresses, dance skirts, wands, jewelry, and other regalia.

SUBSISTENCE AND ECONOMIC STRATEGIES

Hunting, fishing, and the gathering of wild plant foods provided traditional subsistence in native California. In general, men were responsible for the taking of larger animals and for fishing, while women and children gathered plant foods and small game. For their respective activities men made bows and arrows used for both hunting and fishing, as well as other equipment such as throwing sticks, fishing gear, snares, and traps. Women made nets, baskets, and other gathering implements as well as clothing, pots, and cooking utensils.

Food resources varied across the landscape. Shellfish, deep-sea fish, surf fish, acorns, and game were the main subsistence staples for coastal peoples. Groups living in the foothills and valleys relied on acorns, the shoots and seeds of weedy plants and tule (a type of reed), game, fish, and waterfowl. Desert-dwellers sought piñon nuts, mesquite fruit, and game (especially antelope and rabbit) and engaged in some agriculture.

Native Californians developed a variety of specialized technological devices to help them maximize the productivity of the region's diverse environments. The Chumash of southern coastal California made seaworthy plank canoes from which they hunted large sea mammals. Peoples living on bays and lakes used tule rafts, while riverine groups had flat-bottom dugouts made by hollowing out large logs. Traditional food-preservation techniques included drying, hermetic sealing, and the leaching of those foods, notably acorns, that were high in acid content. Milling and grinding equipment was also common.

RELIGIOUS BELIEFS AND PRACTICES

The religious institutions of indigenous California were inextricably bound to its political, economic, social, and legal systems. Two religious systems, the Kuksu in the north and the Toloache in the south, dominated. Priests, shamans, and ritualists led these systems, each of which involved the formal indoctrination of initiates, who had the potential for a series of subsequent status promotions within the religious society. These processes could literally occupy initiates, members, and mentors throughout their lifetimes. Members of these religious societies exercised considerable economic, political, and social influence in the community.

In the Kuksu religion (common among the Pomo, Yuki, Maidu, and Wintun), colourful and dramatic costumes and equipment were used during ritual impersonations of specific spirit-beings. These means were used to enact the myths of the creator and the culture hero, with Coyote and Thunder as the chief characters. Within the Toloache religion (as among the Luiseño and Diegueño), initiates performed while drinking a hallucinogenic decoction made of the jimsonweed plant (*Datura stramonium*). The drug put them in a trance and provided them with supernatural knowledge about their future lives and roles as members of the sacred societies.

Religions on the Colorado River differed slightly because they were not concerned with developing formal organizations and recruitment procedures. Individuals received religious information through dreams, and members recited long narrative texts, explaining the creation of the world, the travel of culture heroes, and the adventures of historic figures.

In the northwestern part of the California culture area, there was another type of informally structured religious system. Its rituals concerned world renewal (as in the white-deerskin dance) and involved the recitation of myths that were privately owned—that is, for which only a few individuals possessed the prerogative of recitation. One communal need served by these ceremonies was the reification (or, sometimes, restructuring) of relationships. The display of costumes and valuable possessions (such as white deerskins or delicately chipped obsidian blades)

A Native American man dressed for the ritualistic white deerskin dance.
Buyenlarge/Archive Photos/Getty Images

reaffirmed social ranking, and the success of the ritual reaffirmed the orderly relationship of humanity to the supernatural.

The use of supernatural power to control events or transform reality was basic to every California group. Generally magic was used in attempts to control the weather, increase the harvest of crops, and foretell the future. Magic or sorcery was deemed not only the cause of sickness and death but also the principal means of curing many diseases. Its practices were also considered to be ways to protect oneself, to punish wrongdoers, and to satisfy personal ends.

SOUL LOSS

In many preliterate cultures, the departure of the soul from the body and its failure to return—a concept known as soul loss—is believed to be a primary cause of illness and death.

In some cultures individuals are believed to have one soul that may wander inadvertently when its owner's guard is relaxed, as when asleep, sneezing, or yawning. Other cultures believe that each person has two or more souls, usually including a "wandering" soul that experiences one's dreams and a "life" soul that maintains one's corporeal vitality. The most dangerous instances of soul loss involve malevolent witchcraft and the enticement and capture of a soul in order to cause harm to its owner.

Those who believe in soul loss hold that an owner can prevent the soul from wandering by means of ritual utterances, such as saying "God bless" when one sneezes, or by a variety of supernatural means, such as the wearing of charms or ingesting of magical substances. However, in cases where the soul's owner believes he or she has been bewitched, soul retrieval requires complex techniques and the services of a religious specialist. The essence of most cures is the catching of the lost soul by a shaman and its reintroduction into the patient's body.

MARRIAGE AND FAMILY

Marriage and the establishment of family units bore great weight when it came to long-term economic and social bonds and obligations within indigenous groups. As such, marriages were virtually always arranged by the families of the prospective bride and groom. Goods were exchanged, with the bulk coming from the husband's family. In most cases the wife took up residence with the husband's family and was taught the ways of the group by her mother-in-law.

Adults of childbearing age were generally responsible for providing food for the group. The generation senior to them—their parents, aunts, and uncles—were typically responsible for raising the children of the community. Learning was a continuous process in which older persons instructed children through elaborate tales containing lessons concerning behaviour and values. Constant supervision, provided by adults, older siblings, and other relatives, reminded younger children about how things should be done.

The educational process became more intense and dramatic during rites of passage, when individuals attained new status and responsibility. The female puberty ritual, for example, generally included a time of isolation, because girls were considered especially empowered (and therefore potentially dangerous on a spiritual level) at menarche. Depending on the tribe, this ritual varied in length from several days to several weeks. During this time an older woman would care for the girl and instruct her in her role as an adult. Initiation ceremonies for boys were less common and, when carried out, were usually less formal, involving instruction in male occupations and behaviour and predictions regarding the boy's future religious, economic, or political career.

Adult education could be heavily institutionalized. Young Chumash men, for instance, purchased apprenticeships from guildlike associations of professional artisans. Young Pomo men were also charged a fee to be trained as apprentices by recognized professional craftsmen, albeit without the intervention of a craft association.

Leaders and specialists continued their training on a less-formal level throughout their lifetimes. A person destined to become chief received instruction from others (such as elders, ritualists, and shamans) and continued to receive such counsel after assumption of office.

ORAL TRADITION AND THE ARTS

Although the elaborate creation tales and epic poems of the Native Californians were the art for which they were most renowned, the documentation of the mythology of the California tribes was thoroughly disrupted by Euro-American colonization, and thus the breadth of the art remains unknown. There were also songs that recounted tales of victory, recent events, daily activities, and romantic love. Songs were usually short but could, in narrative form, last for days. Singing was accompanied by rattles, whistles, or drums.

Visual art forms ranged from decoration on items of daily use, such as baskets

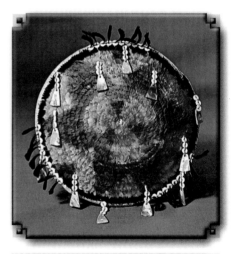

Pomo feathered gift basket decorated with shell pendants, c. 1890; in the National Museum of the American Indian, Heye Foundation, New York City. Courtesy of the Museum of the American Indian, Heye Foundation, New York

and tools, to elaborate rock paintings and rock engravings. Rock paintings were widespread, and, in various parts of the region, designs were incised or pecked into rock surfaces as well. Rock art served a range of functions, from recording individual and group rituals to marking trails.

California peoples were renowned for their exquisite basketwork, though pottery in the eastern desert was also handsomely shaped and decorated. Costuming, particularly in relation to the Kuksu religion, involved the creation of elaborate headdresses, skirts, feathered garments, and other regalia, which were often symbolic of supernatural beings. Painting on the body was also a popular form of adornment.

MISSIONS, COLONIZATION, AND CHANGE

In 1769 the Spanish priest Junípero Serra began to build a series of missions along the region's southern Pacific Coast. Upon their arrival, Serra and his fellow missionaries—who were accompanied by soldiers and soon followed by ranchers and other colonial developers—initiated a long period of cultural rupture for most of California's indigenous peoples. Native communities were often forcibly dislocated to missions, where they were made to work for the colonizers and to convert to Christianity. In less than a century the rest of California had been colonized: in 1812 Russian fur traders founded an outpost at Fort Ross (about 90 miles [140 km] north of present-day San Francisco), and the gold rush that began in 1848 drew some 250,000 Euro-Americans to the California interior over the next five years. Together, these and other events caused the native population to collapse to such an extent—from a precontact high of perhaps 275,000 to perhaps 15,000 in

JUNÍPERO SERRA

(b. Nov. 24, 1713, Petra, Majorca, Spain—d. Aug. 28, 1784, Carmel, California, New Spain [now in U.S.])

The Spanish Franciscan priest Junípero Serra is noted for his missionary work in North America, which earned him (among his admirers) the byname of Apostle of California.

After entering the Franciscan Order in 1730 and being ordained in 1738, Serra taught philosophy at Lullian University, in Palma, on the Spanish island of Majorca. In 1750 he arrived in Mexico City for missionary work among the Indians, serving first in the Sierra Gorda missions from 1750 to 1758 and then in south-central Mexico from 1758 to 1767.

When Spain began its occupation of Alta California (present-day California), Serra joined the expedition's commander, Gaspar de Portolá. On July 16, 1769, he founded Mission San Diego, the first within the present state of California. From 1770 to 1782 he founded eight more Californian missions: Carmel, his headquarters, at Monterey, in 1770; San Antonio and San Gabriel (near Los Angeles), 1771; San Luis Obispo, 1772; San Francisco (Mission Dolores) and San Juan Capistrano, 1776; Santa Clara, 1777; and San Buenaventura, 1782. Serra's missions helped strengthen Spain's control of Alta California.

Serra's treatment of the Indians is debated. His advocates claim that he was a strenuous defender of the Indians and introduced to their lands the cattle, sheep, grains, and fruits of Mexico. Beginning in the 20th century, however, his critics charged him with having enslaved those he converted and with being substantially no different from any other single-minded representative of the colonial system. Serra was beatified on Sept. 25, 1988.

the closing decades of the 19th century—that some have described the period as genocidal.

After a period of intense oversight during the late 19th and early 20th centuries, the U.S. government terminated most of its federal obligations to native Californians in 1955. Indigenous *rancherías*, or reservations, have become relatively autonomous in the period since. Each *ranchería* has an elected body of officials, usually known as a business committee or tribal council, which acts as a liaison between the tribal community and such outside interests as the U.S. Bureau of Indian Affairs, business corporations desiring the purchase or lease of reservation lands, public utilities seeking rights-of-way across lands, and other entities having some form of business with the group. Typically, the council also hears intratribal grievances and participates in planning economic and social development programs.

By the early 21st century, many California Indians were not readily distinguishable from other people residing in California in terms of external factors such as clothing, housing, transportation, or education. However, indigenous attitudes, rituals, and other aspects of traditional culture remained vibrant throughout the state. Many native Californians choose to live in rural areas and reside on reservations. Others choose to live in urban or suburban areas. And still others live part of the year on a reservation and spend the rest of the year in a city or suburb.

Throughout California one finds indigenous ceremonial structures, the continued use and manufacture of ritual materials, and the use of traditional foods. Many art forms, especially basket weaving, continue to be passed from one generation to another, and many native languages, though spoken less and less as first languages, are maintained as part of an overall interest in indigenous heritage. Some *rancherías* have cultural centres and museums that help to preserve their cultures and languages, and in some school districts classes in native languages and cultures are being offered to both children and adults.

Traditional culture is less obvious in the major population centres of the state, which now range along the coast and the Central Valley from San Francisco and Oakland south to San Diego. Native culture has not ceased in urban areas but rather has become an important part of a larger tapestry of urban cultural diversity. Growing at a faster rate than the general population, California's indigenous population is the highest in the United States. Early 21st-century estimates indicated some 630,000 individuals of indigenous descent residing there. Two California cities—Los Angeles and San Diego—are among the 10 U.S. cities with the largest resident populations of Native North Americans.

Not all Native Americans living in California are California Indians, and the growth of this population is a relatively recent phenomenon. People from throughout North America, including indigenous individuals, gravitated to the state in large numbers during World War II in order to work in the burgeoning defense industries of that era. A second wave of native migration to California occurred in the 1950s, during an aggressive indigenous relocation program carried out by the U.S. Bureau of Indian Affairs. However well-intended, the Bureau of Indian Affairs' coordination of the relocation plan—which had been designed to move native individuals and families from job-poor reservations to employment-rich urban areas—was often ineptly carried out and frequently abandoned families once they had relocated. As predominantly rural people finding themselves in unfamiliar urban areas with little of the interfamilial social and economic support to which they were accustomed, many newly urban Native Americans sought each other out and developed independent service and support organizations in the cities.

As a result of these migrations, the unique cultural patterns of the many tribes now represented in California are apparent throughout the state, and there is also a strong pantribal ethos that has fostered city- and statewide recreational, educational, and political groups. For instance, in 1964 a group of Native Americans occupied Alcatraz Island, citing an 1868 treaty allowing them to claim any "unoccupied government land." Although the protestors occupied Alcatraz only for a period of hours, their concerns were later pursued by others: in 1969 a group of approximately 100 individuals calling themselves "Indians of all Tribes" occupied Alcatraz again, this time staying until 1971. The purposes of the occupations were to publicize Indian demands for self-determination, to force negotiations for a Native American cultural centre, museum, and university, and to gain (or, in the occupiers' view, to regain) legal title to the island. In the early 21st century, California's Native American coalitions were continuing to merge political and educational activism and, with organizations such as the American Indian Historical Society and the California Indian Education Association, are assertively examining, criticizing, and providing new teaching materials for schoolteachers who work with indigenous children and for the state curriculum as it regards Native American life and culture.

The peoples of California include representatives of some 20 language families, including Uto-Aztecan, Penutian, Yokutsan, and Athabaskan. American linguist Edward Sapir described California's languages as being more diverse than those found in all of Europe. Among the prominent tribes that have a language named for them are the Hupa, Maidu, Pomo, Wintun, Yana, Yuki, and Yurok. These groups and others are described below.

CAHUILLA

The Cahuilla (Kawia) spoke a Uto-Aztecan language. They originally lived in what is now southern California, in an inland basin of desert plains and rugged canyons south of the San Bernardino and San Jacinto mountains.

The Cahuilla traditionally lived in thatched or adobe houses or in sun shelters without walls and were skilled in basketry and pottery. They based descent on the paternal line and apparently divided into halves, or moieties, which guided such matters as descent and marriage. As with other California Indians, the Cahuilla subsisted on acorns, piñon, elderberries, wild grapes, and several roots and a variety of deer and small game, including rabbit, hare, ground squirrel, hawks, and other birds. These resources tended to be concentrated near water sources, which were unevenly distributed across the desert landscape. Thus, small kin-based bands operated as the typical social unit, with each generally associated with a given subsistence territory.

KATHERINE SIVA SAUBEL

(b. March 7, 1920, Los Coyotes Reservation [on the border of Riverside and San Diego counties], Calif., U.S.)

The Native American scholar and educator Katherine Siva Saubel committed herself early in life to preserving her Cahuilla culture and language, and to promoting their fuller understanding by the larger public.

Reared on the Palm Springs Reservation in California, Katherine Siva was taught by her parents from an early age to honour the traditions of her people, the Cahuilla. After graduating from Palm Springs High School, she worked as a teacher's assistant at the University of California, Los Angeles (1959–60), and as a consultant to linguist Hansjakob Seiler at the University of Cologne, Germany (1964–74). In the process Saubel became a scholar of the history, literature, and culture of the Cahuilla. Together with her husband, historian Mariano Saubel, and others, she cofounded the Malki Museum on the Morongo Indian Reservation in Banning, Calif., which not only displays artifacts dating from prehistoric to recent times but also sponsors the publication of scholarly works on Native Americans from the region.

Saubel's own scholarship had two very different focuses: ethnobotany and the Cahuilla language. In the late 1970s Seiler and Saubel collaborated on both a grammar and a dictionary for Cahuilla, a language that had never before been preserved in writing. She also published a dictionary, *I'Isniyatam (Designs): A Cahuilla Word Book* (1977). An authority also on the unique Cahuilla uses of plants, Saubel was the coauthor, with anthropologist John Lowell Bean, of *Temalpakh (From the Earth): Cahuilla Indian Knowledge and Usage of Plants* (1972) and of two books of ethnobotanical notes. In addition to teaching Cahuilla history, literature, and culture on various campuses in California and at the University of Cologne, Saubel also served on the California Native American Heritage Commission, where her intervention helped preserve locations sacred to Native Americans throughout the state. She was named 1987 Elder of the Year by the California State Indian Museum and was inducted into the National Women's Hall of Fame.

In the 21st century, perhaps the most visible group of Cahuilla was the Agua Caliente band, which operated a tourism centre that includes a hotel and casino. Late 21st-century population estimates indicated more than 3,000 Cahuilla descendants.

CHUMASH

The language of the Chumash is a Hokan language. The people originally lived in what are now the California coastlands and adjacent inland areas from Malibu northward to Estero Bay, and on the three northern Channel Islands off Santa Barbara.

The Chumash were among the first native Californians to be encountered by the Spanish-sponsored explorer Juan Rodríguez Cabrillo (1542–43). At the time of colonization, the Spanish referred to the major Chumash groups as the Obispeño, Purismeño, Ynezeño, Barbareño, and Ventureño (for the Franciscan missions San Luis Obispo de Tolosa, La Purísima Concepción, Santa Ynez, Santa Barbara, and San Buenaventura, respectively), the inland Emigdiano and Cuyama, and the Isleño.

Traditionally, the majority of the Chumash population lived along the seashores and relied for food largely on fish, mollusks, sea mammals, and birds. They also collected a number of wild plant foods. Most important among these were acorns, which the Chumash detoxified using a leaching process. Their houses were dome-shaped and large. Normally each served several families and had several rooms. Villages formed the basis of Chumash political and social organization, and the Chumash based their descent on the maternal line.

The Chumash were skilled artisans. They made plank canoes (*tomol*s) up to 30 feet (9 metres) long as well as a variety of tools out of wood, whalebone, and other

A replica of a redwood plank tomol spirit boat, constructed and intricately carved in the Chumash tradition, on display in Thousand Oaks, Calif. Marilyn Angel Wynn/Native Stock/Getty Images

materials. They also fashioned vessels of soapstone and produced some of the most complex basketry in native North America. In addition, the Chumash were purveyors of clamshell-bead currency for southern California.

Early 21st-century population estimates indicated some 7,000 Chumash descendants.

COSTANOANS

The Costanoans speak a language that is classified as Penutian. They originally lived in an area stretching from the San Francisco Bay region southward to what is now Point Sur, Calif. Traditionally, Costanoans lived in a number of independently organized villages. Quasi-tribal groupings were later imposed on them by Spanish colonizers on the basis of their proximity to various Franciscan missions. Hence, the Costanoans were renamed the Soledad, Monterey, San Juan Bautista, Santa Cruz, Santa Clara (linked with San José), and San Francisco tribes. A group was also named San Pablo, though there was no mission associated with this group.

The chief sources of food for the Costanoans were the sea and streams, which provided mussels, salmon, sea mammals, and seaweed. Rabbits, acorns, and seeds were additional foods. Housing consisted of poles covered with tule (reeds) and brush. For clothing, women wore aprons front and back. Men usually went naked.

Costanoan culture was radically transformed after the establishment of missions, as church-imposed tribal assignments mixed members of alien Indian groups and brought about the destruction of most of their institutions. Costanoan descendants numbered more than 4,500 in the early 21st century.

DIEGUEÑOS

The Diegueños (or San Diegueños) are a group of Yuman-speaking peoples who originally inhabited large areas extending on both sides of what is now the U.S.–Mexican border in California and Baja California. They were named after the mission of San Diego. They call themselves Kumeyaay.

Traditional Diegueño culture reflected similarities with its neighbours the Luiseño to the north and other Yuman nations to the east, such as the Mojave. Their social organization was based upon lineage, with each lineage apparently associated with a particular location. The lineage chief led ceremonies. The dietary staples of coastal Diegueño were fish and mollusks, while inland Diegueño engaged in agriculture. Both inland and coastal groups made baskets, pottery, and containers made of string

MISSION INDIANS

The term "Mission Indians" refers to all the North American Indians of what is now the southern and central California coast, among whom Spanish Franciscans and soldiers established 21 missions between 1769 and 1823. The major groups were, from south to north, the Diegueño, Luiseño and Juaneño, Gabrielino, Chumash, and Costanoan.

The Franciscans had been given two goals by the Spanish crown: to spread Roman Catholicism and to create a docile taxpaying citizenry for New Spain. However, beyond some instruction in the Spanish language, Christian dogma, and hymn singing, the aboriginal peoples received little formal education. They were put to work tending mission farms, livestock, and facilities and discouraged—in some cases prohibited—from leaving their home mission. Many were converted, many died of European diseases to which they had no immunity, and many became dependent upon the missions for subsistence and shelter.

When the authority of the missions was officially ended by the Mexican government in 1834, many of the tribes were left adrift. By law they were promised the rights of citizenship and one-half of all former mission property, but many were exploited and despoiled by speculators. Others successfully assimilated into the Mexican system. In the 20th century some Mission tribes became relatively wealthy through the sale and lease of their land-holdings in resort areas such as the Cahuilla in Palm Springs, Calif.

substances. Their houses consisted of poles supporting a roof of brush and earth.

Although many Diegueño religious practices paralleled those of the Luiseño, the world views of the two differed. Whereas the Luiseño were mystics, the Diegueño were more interested in the solid and visible in life. Like most other California Indians, the Diegueño resisted the Christianizing efforts of the Spanish.

Diegueño descendants numbered more than 3,500 in the early 21st century.

GABRIELINO

The name Gabrielino (Gabrieleño), or San Gabrielino, refers to any of two, or possibly three, dialectally and culturally related North American Indian groups who spoke a language of Uto-Aztecan stock and lived in the lowlands, along the seacoast, and on islands in southern California at the time of Spanish colonization. The Gabrielino proper, who call themselves Tongva, inhabited what are now southern and eastern Los Angeles County and northern Orange County, as well as the islands of Santa Catalina and San Clemente. They were named by the Spanish after the Franciscan mission San Gabriel Arcángel. The second group, Tataviam (Fernandeño), occupied areas in and around the San Fernando Valley and seacoast. A third, apparently related, group was the Nicolino (Nicoleño, or San Nicolinos), who inhabited San Nicolas Island.

The Gabrielino occupied some of the most fertile and pleasant land in California. Because they were among the wealthiest and most technologically advanced Native Americans in the region, they exercised considerable influence on all their neighbours. In religion, for instance, the Gabrielino were the source of the jimsonweed cult, a widely practiced southern California religion that involved various sacred and esoteric rituals and the drinking of toloache, a hallucinogen made from the jimsonweed (*Datura stramonium*).

Traditionally, the interior and coastal Gabrielino lived in houses constructed of poles and tule-reed mats. Their economy was based on acorns and other wild plant foods, supplemented by fishing and hunting. Island Gabrielino, especially the Nicolino, often built dwellings of whale ribs covered with sea-lion skins or brush, and for food they relied on fish, sea mammals and birds, and mollusks. All groups made baskets, and a quarry on Santa Catalina Island provided soapstone that tribal members made into such items as pots and scoops, ceremonial vessels, artistic carvings, beads, and ornaments. Trade between islanders, coastal people, and interior residents was extensive and based on a currency of clamshell beads. Each Gabrielino village had a hereditary chief. Shamanism was an important part of Gabrielino religion and healing practices.

Early 21st-century population estimates indicated some 2,000 Gabrielino descendants.

HUPA

A cultural combination of both Northwest Coast and California Indians, the Hupa, who spoke a variant of the Athabaskan language, lived in villages located on the bank of the lower Trinity River in what is now the state of California. There were dwellings built specifically for women and children, while men slept and took sweat baths in separate semisubterranean buildings; women also had small menstrual lodges.

The Hupa economy was based on elk, deer, salmon, and acorns, all of which were readily available in the region. Fine basketry was made by twining segments of certain roots, leaves, and stems around prepared shoots. As an inland group, the Hupa often exchanged acorns and other local foods with the coast-dwelling Yurok, who reciprocated with redwood canoes, saltwater fish, mussels, and seaweed. Members of the two tribes attended each other's ceremonies and sometimes intermarried.

Hupa people traditionally measured wealth in terms of the ownership of woodpecker scalps and dentalium shells, the latter of which were probably received in trade from

A Hupa man preparing to spear fish in a stream during the early years of the 20th century. Buyenlarge/Archive Photos/Getty Images

the Yurok. The village's richest man was its headman. His power and his property passed to his son, but anyone who acquired more property might obtain the dignity and power of that office. Personal insult, injury, or homicide were usually settled through the payment of blood money.

The recitation of magical formulas was an important part of traditional Hupa religion. Shamanism was also common. Shamans' fees were paid in dentalium shells or deerskin blankets. Three major dances were held annually for the benefit of the community, as were spring and fall ceremonial feasts.

Early 21st-century population estimates indicated more than 3,000 Hupa descendants.

LUISEÑO

The Luiseño, who called themselves Payomkowishum, spoke a Uto-Aztecan language and inhabited a region extending from what is now Los Angeles to San Diego, Calif. Some of the group were named Luiseño after the Mission San Luis Rey de Francia. Others were called Juaneño because of their association with the Mission San Juan Capistrano. Early ethnographers classified the two into separate cultures, but they are now regarded as one group.

Although some Luiseño lived on the Pacific coast, where they fished and gathered mollusks, the great majority lived in the inland hills and valleys. As with many other California Indians, they subsisted on acorns, seeds, fruits, and roots as well as game hunted with bows and arrows or snares. In the warm climate the men wore nothing, and the women wore an apron front and back.

Luiseño lived in villages of semisubterranean earth-covered lodges and were apparently organized in small kin-based groups clustered into clans or quasi-clans.

These had territorial, political, and economic functions. Everyone belonged to religious societies, which had both ceremonial and political functions. Several family groupings had chiefs, and in most areas there was apparently a chief of chiefs.

The Luiseño were mystics, and their conception of a great, all-powerful, avenging god was uncommon for aboriginal North America. In deference to this god, Chingichnish, they held a series of initiation ceremonies for boys, some of which involved a drug made from jimsonweed (*Datura stramonium*). This was drunk to inspire visions or dreams of the supernatural, which were central to the Luiseño religion. Equally important were mourning ceremonies, a series of funerary observances and anniversary commemorations of the dead. Shamans and medicine men were important in curing disease.

Population estimates indicated approximately 9,000 Juaneño and Luiseño descendants in the early 21st century.

MAIDU

The Maidu spoke a language of Penutian stock and originally lived in a territory extending eastward from the Sacramento River to the crest of the Sierra Nevada mountains and centring chiefly in the drainage of the Feather and American rivers in California.

The Maidu ate seeds and acorns and hunted elk, deer, bears, rabbits, ducks, and geese, as did several other tribes of California Indians. They also fished for salmon, lamprey eel, and other river life. Before Spanish colonization, each Maidu group resided in one of three habitats: the inland valleys, the Sierra Nevada foothills, or the mountains themselves. The valley people were prosperous, but poverty was more common in the higher habitats. Ironically, those Maidu who were the least exposed to inclement conditions had the most-sophisticated technology and were able to construct the most-protective shelter. Thus, the valley people built large earth-covered communal dwellings, whereas the foothill dwellers and mountaineers made more-fragile brush or bark lean-tos.

Traditional Maidu social organization was built around autonomous, yet allied, settlements. Each claimed a communal territory and acted as a single political unit. Among southern groups the chiefs were hereditary, but among northern groups they could be deposed and probably achieved their position through wealth and popularity.

Like many other central California tribes, the Maidu practiced the Kuksu religion, involving male secret societies, rites, masks and disguises, and special earth-roofed ceremonial chambers. Some of the purposes of the rituals were naturalistic—to ensure good crops or plentiful game or to ward off floods and other natural disasters, such as disease.

Population estimates indicated more than 4,000 individuals of Maidu descent in the early 21st century.

MIWOK

The Miwok (Mewuk) spoke languages of Penutian stock and originally comprised seven dialectally and territorially discrete branches: the Coast Miwok in an area just north of what is now San Francisco; the Lake Miwok in the Clear Lake Basin; the Bay Miwok (or Saclan), living along the delta of the San Joaquin and Sacramento rivers; the Plains Miwok, living farther up the lower Sacramento and San Joaquin rivers; and, just eastward, three groups of Sierra Miwok—Northern, Central, and Southern—in the western foothills of the Sierra Nevada. The Sierra branches constituted the greatest number of Miwok individuals and had more than 100 villages at the time of European contact.

Traditionally, the groups near and on the coast—the Coast, Lake, and Bay Miwok—gathered acorns, fished, and hunted deer and other game with bow and arrow. They lived in semisubterranean pole- and earth-covered lodges and produced watertight basketry ornamented with beads or feathers. The interior Miwok—those of the Sierra and Plains—resided in the foothills and lowlands and generally moved into the high sierras only for summer hunting. Their main abodes were also semisubterranean earth-covered houses, while their mountain shelters were temporary lean-tos of bark over a sapling framework. Their chief food staple was acorns, which were stored in basketlike granaries. The interior Miwok also partook in the Kuksu cult, which included various rituals, costumed dances using animal skins, and impersonations of spirits.

Traditional Miwok society was organized into contrasting halves, or moieties, each with several lineages. The moieties controlled both kinship and politics, regulating such matters as descent, marriage, and relations with other tribes. Each moiety had chiefs and subchiefs, positions that were open to both men and women.

Miwok descendants numbered more than 5,700 in the early 21st century.

MONO

The name Mono (Monachi) may be applied to either of two groups, originally from what is now central California, who spoke a language belonging to the Numic group of the Uto-Aztecan family and were related to the Northern Paiute. The Western Mono, who resided in the pine belt of the Sierra Nevada mountains, had a culture similar to that of the nearby Yokuts. The Owens Valley Paiute (previously called the Eastern Mono) were more similar to their neighbours from the Great Basin culture area.

Historically, the two divisions traded with each other, the Owens Valley Paiute exchanging salt, piñon nuts, baskets, and poison in return for acorn flour, baskets, and shafts for arrows.

Traditional Mono social organization consisted of small villages of as many as 50 to 75 people, organized in patrilineal families and ranging over loosely defined hunting areas. Although the power of the chief was far from absolute, his consent was required for all major religious or warlike undertakings. His greatest responsibilities were the settlement of disputes and the sanctioning of punishment.

Early 21st-century population estimates indicated some 3,000 Mono descendants.

POMO

The Pomo are Hokan-speaking peoples of the West Coast of the United States. Their territory was centred in the Russian River Valley some 50 to 100 miles (80 to 160 km) north of what is now San Francisco. Pomo territory also included the adjacent coastlands and the interior highlands near Clear Lake. A small detached group lived in the Sacramento River Valley surrounded by Wintun people.

Traditionally, the Pomo were a comparatively wealthy people, well supplied with food and other natural resources. Fish, waterfowl, deer, acorns, bulb plants, seeds, and other wild foods were plentiful. Northeastern Pomo settlements held a lucrative salt deposit, and southeastern settlements had magnesite, a substance that was combined with ground shells and made into the beads that were used as standard currency in north-central California. Pomo basketry, considered by some to be the finest in California, was exceptionally well twined and intricately ornamented, using various woody materials, beads, and

The Pomo are known for their basket-weaving skills. Their baskets were tightly woven and frequently featured colourful ornamentation such as beads and feathers. Buyenlarge/Archive Photos/Getty Images

coloured feathers. Pomo housing varied with the locale: coastal residents constructed dwellings of heavy timber and bark, and inland peoples built various types of dwellings out of such materials as poles, brush, grass, and tule mats. Traditional Pomo religion involved the Kuksu cult, which involved private ceremonies and esoteric dances and rituals.

Early 21st-century population estimates indicated approximately 8,000 individuals of Pomo descent.

SERRANO

The Serrano spoke a Uto-Aztecan language and originally inhabited a mountainous region of what is now southern California. *Serrano* means "mountain dweller" in Spanish. Their name for themselves is *Yuhaviatam*

(Yuharetum), which means "people of the pines." One band, the Kitanemuk, lived in the Kern and San Joaquin river basins. Another band, the Vanyume, resided along the Mojave River. A third, the Serrano proper, held the San Bernardino Mountains, adjacent valleys, and a portion of the Mojave Desert.

All three bands were hunting and gathering cultures that knew how to subsist in a difficult environment. Small game, acorns, piñon nuts, and berries were their dietary staples. Within villages the people were organized into patrilineal clans, with each clan having a hereditary chief and assistant chief. Dwellings were wickiups (wigwams), circular domed structures of willow branches covered with tule (rush) thatching. Most villages also had a ceremonial house where the chief lived, as well as a heated sweat lodge for bathing and ritual purification.

Early 21st-century population estimates indicated some 500 individuals of Serrano descent.

SHASTA

The Shasta spoke related languages of Hokan stock and lived in the highlands of what is now interior northern California and southern Oregon, in the basins of the Upper Klamath, the Scott, and the Shasta rivers. Their main subdivisions were the Shasta Valley Shasta, the Scott Valley Shasta, and the Klamath River Shasta. Others included the New River Shasta, Konomihu, and Okwanuchu. Formerly included with the Shasta but now often classified separately are the Achomawi and Atsugewi.

Traditional Shasta life was similar to but more difficult than that of the neighbouring Yurok, as Shasta villages were generally confined to narrow ridges of canyons, and their food supply was less plentiful. Like the Yurok and Karok, the Shasta subsisted largely on acorns and salmon and traded with other northern California Indians, using such currency as dentalium shells and scarlet woodpecker scalps. Shasta villages, dwellings, and communal sweat houses were similar to those of other tribes in the region, though Shasta men were inclined to put up their own individual sweat houses in addition to the communal structure. Shasta religion centred on guardian spirits and shamanism.

In the 21st century, the Shasta were one of 17 tribes that composed the Confederated Tribes of Siletz Indians. Early 21st-century population estimates indicated some 1,000 individuals of Shasta descent.

WINTUN

The Wintun consist of a number of groups of Penutian-speaking peoples who originally inhabited the west side of the Sacramento Valley in what is today California. Their traditional territory was some 250 miles (400 km) from north to south and included stretches of the flanking foothills. Four primary linguistic groupings, each including a number of dialects, made up the Wintun population: the northern Wintun (Wintu), the central Wintun (Nomlaki), and the two subdivisions of the southern Wintun, the Hill and River Patwin. The Patwin are sometimes classified as a group separate from the Wintun.

The elongated shape of Wintun territory made for considerable cultural diversity. Before colonization by the Spanish, contacts with close neighbours to the east and west were more frequent for most communities than were those with other Wintun at the extremities of the territory. In the north, for instance, basketry was twined in the fashion of the Oregon Indians. In the centre it was intricately ornamented like that of the Pomo. And in the south it had mixed characteristics. Similarly, Wintun houses varied by region: River Patwin houses were earth-covered domes while Hill Patwin used conical bark structures and simpler thatched dwellings. The nature of the northern groups' houses is unknown. Wintun economies relied upon wild foods, including acorns, fish, and waterfowl. Extended family groups composed autonomous tribelets, and they lived in permanent villages near rivers and streams. The Patwin, however, are known to have had a community chief with near-absolute power.

Wintun religion was based on the belief in a single creator. The southern Wintun greatly influenced the development of the Kuksu cult, a religion of secret societies and rituals that spread to a number of California tribes. The cult's main purposes were to bring strength to young male initiates, to bring fertility to natural crops, and to ward off natural disasters.

There were at least 12,000 Wintun before the Spanish colonization of California. Epidemics of Old World diseases (to which the Wintun had no immunity) greatly reduced their numbers, as did violence resulting from California's mid-19th-century gold rush. Wintun descendants numbered more than 3,800 in the early 21st century.

YANA

The Yana spoke a Hokan language and lived along the eastern tributaries of the upper Sacramento River, from the Pit River to southwest of Lassen Peak, in what is now California. Traditional Yana territory comprised a myriad of foothills and narrow, rugged canyons, partly wooded but mostly brush-covered and rocky.

Before colonization there were four Yana divisions— Northern, Central, and Southern Yana, as well as Yahi—speaking mutually intelligible dialects. A significant characteristic of Yana speech was its use of separate forms for men and women. The differences were small, but females used their word forms exclusively, whereas men used the male forms among themselves and the so-called female forms when addressing women.

Life generally was very difficult in the harsh, barren environment. The Yana lived in earth-covered winter lodges and thatch-covered summer dwellings, hunted various game, and fished for salmon. Little is known of their social organization, except that it probably comprised small bands and contained classes or rankings. Before colonization the Yana had relatively frequent skirmishes with their neighbours, an unusual trait for California Indians.

In 1864 the tribe was the victim of particularly brutal attacks by nearby miners. The miners launched an overt campaign of extermination, and over the course of several days they killed all but about 50 of the estimated 3,000 tribal members. The survivors subsequently avoided contact with Euro-Americans by living in isolated canyons. From 1911 until his death in 1916, the last known survivor of the Yahi band, Ishi, worked to record his memories of traditional culture with anthropologist A.L. Kroeber.

Early 21st-century population estimates indicated some 100 Yana descendants.

YUKI

The Yuki comprised four groups of Indians who lived in the Coast Ranges and along the coast of what is now northwestern California. They spoke distinctive languages that are unaffiliated with any other known language. The four Yuki groups were the Yuki-proper, who lived along the upper reaches of the Eel River and its tributaries; the Huchnom of Redwood Valley to the west; the Coast Yuki, who were distributed farther westward along the redwood coast; and the Wappo, who occupied an enclave among the Pomo, some 40 miles (65 km) southward in the Russian River Valley.

Only the linguistic identification links the Wappo with other Yuki. Wappo cultural traditions were otherwise like those of the Pomo. The other Yuki groups were traditionally organized into tribelets, communities composed of several scattered settlements or villages occupying a particular area. Each settlement had its own chief, and there was also a head chief for the community as a whole. There were also a war leader, a person in charge of religious dances, and a shaman, or medicine man or woman. Warfare was apparently frequent between certain communities, between the different Yuki groups, and with other California Indians. The Coast Yuki were an exception, usually maintaining friendly relations with their neighbours. Trade was prevalent among all groups, inland people trading such items as furs with coastal groups, who in turn plied a variety of seafood and shells. Clamshell beads were used as currency.

Yuki (Wappo) ceremonial basket. Photos.com/Jupiterimages

38

The Yuki economy was based on gathering acorns, fishing, mostly for salmon, and hunting such animals as bear and deer. The Coast Yuki relied somewhat more on seafood than the other groups. Interior groups lived in domed earth-covered houses. Coast Yuki had conical houses covered with bark. All had large dance houses and sweat houses.

Traditional Yuki religious beliefs centred generally on two contrasting deities—a creator, whose actions were essentially well intended, and another deity, sometimes associated with thunder, who might help but might also blunder or do evil. Usually the creator was the supreme god of the two, but among the Coast Yuki he had disappeared and only Thunder remained. All Yuki had a great array of ceremonies, rituals, and initiations.

Early 21st-century population estimates indicated some 600 Yuki descendants.

YUROK

The Yurok lived in what is now California along the lower Klamath River and the Pacific coast. They spoke an Algic language and were culturally and linguistically related to the Wiyot. As their traditional territory lay on the border between divergent cultural and ecological areas, the Yurok combined the typical subsistence practices of Northwest Coast Indians with many religious and organizational features common to California Indians.

Traditional Yurok villages were small collections of independent houses owned by individual families. Avoiding unified communities and an overall political authority, village residents sometimes shared rights to general subsistence areas and to the performance of certain rituals. Other rights, such as the right to use specific areas for fishing, hunting, and gathering, generally belonged to

Yurok man with canoe on the lower Klamath River, California; photograph by Edward S. Curtis, c. 1923. Edward S. Curtis Collection/ Library of Congress, Washington, D.C. (Digital file no. cph 3c18588)

particular houses. These rights were acquired by inheritance or dowry, as part of blood money settlements, or by sale. In addition to dwellings, villages had sweat houses, each of which served as a gathering place for the men of an extended patrilineal family. There were also separate shelters to which women retired during menstruation.

The traditional Yurok economy focused on salmon and acorns. The people also produced excellent basketry and made canoes from redwood trees, selling them to inland tribes. Wealth was counted in strings of dentalium shells, obsidian blades, woodpecker scalps, and albino deerskins. Acquiring wealth was an important goal in Yurok culture. Feuds were common, and payments of blood money were precisely defined according to the seriousness of the offense. The value of a man's life depended on his social status.

Traditional Yurok religion was concerned with an individual's effort to elicit supernatural aid, especially through ritual cleanliness, and with rituals for the public welfare. The tribe did not practice the potlatch, masked dances, representative carving, and other features typical of their Northwest Coast neighbours. The major ceremonies were those of the World Renewal cycle, which ensured an abundance of food, riches, and general well-being. This cycle included the recitation of magical formulas, repeating the words of an ancient spirit race, and other acts. The spiritual power to cure disease was granted only to women, giving these shamans prestige and a source of wealth.

Early 21st-century population estimates indicated some 6,000 individuals of Yurok descent.

Chapter 3
GREAT BASIN INDIANS

The indigenous peoples who inhabited the traditional culture area comprising almost all of the present-day states of Utah and Nevada as well as substantial portions of Oregon, Idaho, Wyoming, and Colorado and smaller portions of Arizona, Montana, and California are known as the Great Basin Indians. Great Basin topography includes many small basin and range systems and parts of the mountains, high desert, and low desert that define its external boundaries. The region's northern basin and range systems transition rather gradually to the intermontane plateaus of Idaho and Oregon. Likewise, the differences between the Great Basin Indians and the Plateau Indians are culturally continuous. Anthropologists sometimes refer to the Plateau and Great Basin jointly as the Intermontane culture area.

The Great Basin is arid to semiarid, with annual average precipitation ranging from as little as 2.1 inches (53 mm) in Death Valley to 20–25 inches (500–630 mm) in mountainous areas. Precipitation falls primarily in the form of snow, especially in the high country. Because of the surrounding topography, water does not leave the basin except by evaporation or industrial means. Brackish and even salty water are common on basin floors, as at the Great Salt Lake. The area is characterized by a vertical succession of ecological zones, each with a dominant xerophytic (desert-type) flora and related fauna. Before industrialization, the region's population density was sparse, ranging from 0.8 to 11.7 persons per 100 square miles.

CULTURAL CHARACTERISTICS

Among the elements that distinguish one culture area from another are the languages spoken, the foods eaten, the tools used, the religious beliefs practiced, the clothing worn, and the houses inhabited. At the region's boundaries, many features shade into those of adjoining culture areas.

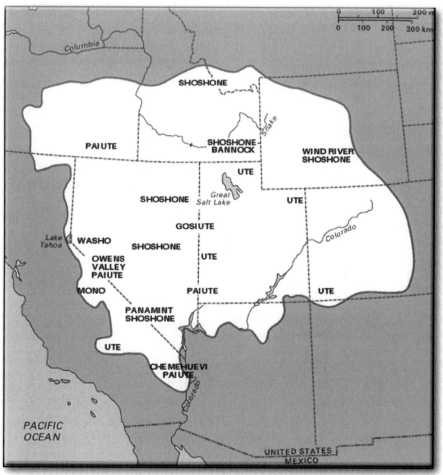

Distribution of Numic languages and major groups of Great Basin–area Indians.

LANGUAGE

Originally, peoples speaking two widely divergent languages occupied the Great Basin region. The Washoe, whose territory centred on Lake Tahoe, spoke a Hokan language related to those spoken in parts of what are now California, Arizona, and Baja California, Mex. The remainder of the Great Basin was occupied by speakers of Numic languages. (The Numic branch is a division of the Uto-Aztecan language family, a group of related languages widely distributed in the western United States and Mexico.) Linguists distinguish Western, Central, and Southern branches of Numic.

HOKAN LANGUAGES

The Hokan languages form a major group, or phylum, of American Indian languages. They are basically agglutinative in structure. That is, they frequently use affixes (such as prefixes and suffixes), as well as compound words, to form long words made up of several elements. Sometimes such words become so complex that a complete sentence or phrase may be expressed by one word. When this occurs, and when the units that compose such a word are "bound" forms (i.e., cannot be used except in conjunction with other elements within a word), the process has gone beyond agglutination and is called polysynthesis, a process characteristic of many American Indian languages. Some Hokan languages are extremely polysynthetic, among them the Yana language of northern California. The Yana word *yābanaumawildjigummaha'nigi* means "let us, each one [of us], move indeed to the west across [the creek]." It is composed of the following elements—*yā* "several people move," *banauma* "everybody," *wil* "across," *dji* "to the west," *gumma* "indeed," *ha'* "let us," and *nigi* "we." Such word sentences are not uncommon in American Indian languages but are by no means universal.

Western Numic languages are spoken by the Owens Valley Paiute (Eastern Mono), several Northern Paiute groups, and the Bannock. Central Numic languages are spoken by the Panamint (Koso) and several Shoshone groups, including the Gosiute, Timbisha, Western Shoshone, and Comanche. Although they originated in the Great Basin, the Comanche acquired horses during the early colonial period, moved to present-day Texas, and became nomadic buffalo hunters. They are thus typically regarded as Plains Indians.

Southern Numic languages are spoken by the Kawaiisu and a number of Ute and Southern Paiute groups, including the Chemehuevi. The distinction between Southern Paiute and Ute is cultural rather than linguistic. Ute speakers who had horses in the early historic period are regarded as Ute, and those who did not readily adopt horses are regarded as Southern Paiute.

The Numic peoples called themselves Numa, Nungwu, or Numu, meaning "people" or "human beings." The various tribal names such as Paiute and Shoshone were designations given them by other tribes. The Washoe called themselves Washoe, a true self-name. Linguistic and archaeological evidence indicates that the Washoe separated from other California Hokan-speaking groups as long as several millennia ago. Similar evidence indicates that the Numic peoples may have been spreading across the Great Basin from southeastern California for the last 2,000 years, reaching their northernmost areas less than 1,000 years ago.

TRANSPORTATION, SHELTER, TOOLS, AND SUBSISTENCE

People inhabited the Great Basin region for thousands of years before horses were introduced, though the acceptance or rejection of the horse is often the standard way of characterizing Great Basin cultures. Groups that used the horse generally occupied the northern and eastern sections of the culture area. The Southern Ute and Eastern Shoshone were among the first peoples north of the Spanish settlements of New Mexico to obtain horses, perhaps by the mid-1600s. These bands subsequently acted as middlemen in the transmission of horses and horse culture from New Mexico to the northern Plains. As the Northern Shoshone of Idaho obtained horses in the 18th century, they were joined by Northern Paiute speakers from eastern Oregon and northern Nevada to form the Shoshone-Bannock bands of historic times. By 1800 the Southern and Northern Ute, the Ute of central Utah, the Eastern Shoshone, the Lemhi Shoshone, and the Shoshone-Bannock had large herds of horses, used tepees or grass-covered domed wickiups, and were increasingly oriented toward the tribes and practices found on the Plains. Bison became their major prey animal, and they began to engage more heavily in the kinds of intertribal trade and warfare characteristic of the Plains Indians.

The tribes to the south and west in the Great Basin proper and on the western Colorado Plateau did not take up the general use of horses until 1850–60. The Washoe did not use horses prior to colonial settlement in the region and rarely used them thereafter. The Numu and the Washoe built two types of shelters: semicircular brush windbreaks in the summer and domed brush, bark-slab, grass, or reed-mat wickiups in the winter. Whether equestrian or pedestrian, Great Basin peoples generally sited their winter villages along the edge of valley floors near water and firewood. Their summer encampments were moved frequently so as not to exhaust the food resources in any given locale.

A Shoshone man on horseback at the beginning of the 20th century. The eastern Shoshone were among the first Great Basin Indians to obtain and utilize horses. Hulton Archive/Getty Images

Aside from horse-related technology, such as halters and saddles, the tools of equestrians and pedestrians were quite similar and very typical of hunting and gathering cultures: the bow and arrow, stone knife, rabbit stick, digging stick, basket, net, and flat seed-grinding slab and hand stone. Some Western Shoshone, Southern Paiute, and Southern Ute groups made a coarse brownware pottery. Some Northern Shoshone made steatite jars and cups. Lines and hooks, harpoons, nets, and willow fish weirs were used on rivers and lakes. Rodents were taken with snares and traps or pulled from burrows with long hooked sticks. Rabbits were driven into nets and clubbed or were shot with bows and arrows. Rabbit drives provided an occasion for people to congregate and socialize, gamble, dance, and court. Antelope were driven into corrals and traps. Waterfowl were netted, trapped, or shot with arrows that had rounded heads and were intended to stun the bird. Some groups made decoys of tule reeds covered with duck skins. Deer, elk, and mountain sheep were taken by individual hunters with bows and arrows or in traps or deadfalls.

Great Basin peoples followed an annual round that encompassed several ecological zones, exploiting plant and animal resources as they became available. Typically, more than 70 percent of the food supply was vegetal. More than 200 species of plants were named and used, principally seed and root plants. Pedestrian groups gathered nuts from piñon pine groves in the upland areas of Nevada and central Utah each autumn, storing large quantities for winter use. Early spring was a difficult time, as such resources were often exhausted, plants immature, and prey animals lean and wary. Some Southern Paiute bands practiced limited horticulture along the Colorado

Petroglyphs located in the Paria Canyon–Vermilion Cliffs Wilderness Area, near the Arizona-Utah border. © Carol Jean Smetana

and Virgin rivers, and some bands of Owens Valley Paiute, Northern Paiute, and Western Shoshone irrigated patches of wild seed plants to increase their yield. Groups with large lakes in their territories did considerable fishing, especially during spawning runs.

Like the pedestrian peoples of the Great Basin, the horse-using groups followed an annual round. However, the latter were able to range over a much larger area than those on foot. They hunted bison, deer, elk, and mountain sheep and collected seed and root foods as these became available. After autumn bison hunts on the northern Plains, groups returned to the Bridger Basin, the Snake River area, or the Colorado mountains for the winter. Shoshone and Shoshone-Bannock peoples caught salmon during the annual spawning run each spring. Fresh salmon was an important food source after the long winter, and some salmon was also dried or smoked for later use. Certain kinds of roots, and especially camas, were also an important food source, although the latter's onionlike bulbs required detoxifying by pit roasting or steaming.

Clothing for those groups that did not use horses consisted of sage bark aprons and breechcloths, augmented by rabbit-skin robes in the winter. Their artistic efforts were often expressed through fine basketry and rock art (petroglyphs and pictographs). The horse-using peoples wore Plains-style tailored skin garments. Like their Plains trade partners, these groups painted their tepees, rawhide shields, and bags and containers, as well as decorating clothing and other soft goods with dyed porcupine quills and, later, glass beads.

Traditionally, western Great Basin groups engaged in trade involving shells (including marine shells), tanned hides, baskets, and foodstuffs. Horse-using groups actively traded among themselves and with others, including fur traders. Shoshone clothing was particularly prized in trade for its beauty and durability. Between about 1800 and 1850, mounted Ute and Navajo bands preyed on Southern Paiute, Western Shoshone, and Gosiute bands for slaves, capturing and sometimes trading women and children to be sold in the Spanish settlements of New Mexico and southern California.

Social Conditions

Pedestrian bands of the Great Basin were organized in a manner that reflects the rather difficult arid environment in which they lived. Groups were typically small, moved frequently, and had a fluid membership. These mobile bands exploited a given territory on a seasonal basis, availing themselves of the available food resources within a particular valley and its adjacent mountains. Food supplies were seldom adequate enough for large groups to remain together for more than a few days. Larger gatherings met only for certain brief periods—for example, during rabbit drives in the spring or during the piñon nut season in the autumn. Where conditions allowed, as for the Washoe at Lake Tahoe and the Northern Paiute and Ute groups at lakes in their districts, people would also aggregate when fish were spawning. These periodic gatherings are perhaps best understood as aggregations of several extended families. They involved no sustained sense of political cohesion.

The same fluidity of social organization was characteristic of the equestrian bands. Possession of horses permitted larger numbers of people to remain together for much of the year, but this did not lead to the development of formal political hierarchies within the tribes. Among both equestrian and pedestrian groups, a particular leader was followed as long as he was successful in leading people to food or in war. If he failed, people would simply join other bands or form new ones.

KINSHIP, MARRIAGE, AND FAMILY

Family was something of a cooperative affair for indigenous peoples of the Great Basin. The basic social unit within this culture area was typically a two- or three-generation family or the nuclear families of two brothers, augmented occasionally by other individuals with ties to the core group. Kin ties were reckoned both maternally and paternally, and were widely extended to distant relatives. This enabled people to invoke the customs of hospitality that rested upon them in order to move from one group to another if circumstances warranted.

Marriage practices varied across the culture area, with a tendency among some groups to marry true cross-cousins (mother's brother's or father's sister's child) or pseudo cross-cousins (mother's brother's or father's sister's stepchild). Both the sororate (marriage between a widower and his dead wife's sister) and the levirate (marriage between a widow and her dead husband's brother) were practiced, as were their logical extensions, sororal polygyny and fraternal polyandry. Although polygynous marriages were formally recognized by communities, polyandry was usually informal, consisting only of a couple extending sexual privileges to the husband's brother for a limited period of time.

There was no set pattern of postmarital residence. A newly married couple might live with the bride's family for the first few years until children were born, but the availability of food supplies was the key factor in determining residence. Marriages could be brittle, especially between young adults. Divorce was easy and socially acceptable. Nonetheless, the difficult environment favoured a division of labour that led most individuals to be married (whether to one person or in a series of partnerships) during most of their adult lives.

Children began to learn about and participate in the food quest while very young. Grandparents were responsible for most caregiving and for teaching children appropriate behaviour and survival skills. Adults of child-bearing age were engaged in providing most of the food for the group. There was little emphasis on puberty rites except among the Washoe, who held a special dance and put a girl through various tests at the time of menarche.

RELIGIOUS BELIEFS AND PRACTICES

A mythical cosmogony, beliefs in powerful spirit-beings, and a belief in a dualistic soul comprise the main religious concepts of this region. Mythology provided a theory of origins in which anthropomorphic animal progenitors, notably Wolf, Coyote, Rabbit, Bear, and Mountain Lion, were supposed to have lived before the human age. During that period they were able to speak and act as humans do. They created the world and were responsible for present-day topography, ecology, food resources, seasons of the year, and distribution of tribes. They set the nature of social relations—that is, they defined how various classes of kin should behave toward each other—and set the customs surrounding birth, marriage, puberty, and death. Their actions in the mythic realm set moral and ethical precepts and determined the physical and behavioral characteristics of the modern animals. Most of the motifs and tale plots of Great Basin mythology arc found widely throughout North America.

Spirit-beings were animals, birds, or natural or supernatural phenomena, each thought to have a specific power according to an observed characteristic. Some such beings were thought to be benevolent, or at least neutral, toward humans. Others, such as water babies—small long-haired creatures who lured people to their death in springs or lakes and who ate children—were malevolent and feared. Great Basin peoples also had conceptions of a variety of other beings, such as the Southern Paiute *unupits*, mischievous spirits who caused illness.

Shamanism was prominent in all Great Basin groups. Both men and women might become shamans. One was called to shamanism by a spirit-being who came unsought. It was considered dangerous to resist this call, for those who did sometimes died. The being became a tutelary guide, instructing an individual in curing and sources of power. Some shamans had several tutelary spirit-beings, each providing instruction for specific practices, such as the power to cure disease, to foretell the future, or to practice sorcery. Among Northern Paiute and Washoe and probably elsewhere, a person who had received power became an apprentice to an older, practicing shaman and from that mentor learned a variety of rituals, cures, and feats of legerdemain associated with curing performances. Curing ceremonies were performed with family members and others present and might last several days. The widespread Native American practice of sucking an object said to cause the disease from the patient's body was often employed. Shamans who lost too many patients were sometimes killed.

In the western Great Basin, some men were thought to have powers to charm antelope and so led communal antelope drives. Beliefs that some men were arrow-proof (and, after the introduction of guns, bulletproof) are reported for the Northern Paiute and Gosiute but were probably general throughout the area. Among the Eastern Shoshone, young men sought contact with spirit-beings by undertaking the vision quest. The Eastern Shoshone probably learned this practice from their Plains neighbours, although the characteristics of the beings sought were those common to Great Basin beliefs.

VISION QUEST

One significant rite of passage for many Native Americans was (and, for some, remains) the vision quest, a supernatural experience in which an individual seeks to interact with a guardian spirit, usually an anthropomorphized animal, to obtain advice or protection.

The specific techniques for attaining visions varied from tribe to tribe, as did the age at which the first quest was to be undertaken, its length and intensity, and the expected form of the guardian spirit's presence or sign. In some tribes nearly all young people traditionally engaged in some form of vision quest, as participation in the experience was one of the rituals marking an individual's transition from childhood to adulthood. In other groups vision questing was undertaken only by males, with menarche and childbirth as the analogous experiences for females.

Usually an individual's first vision quest was preceded by a period of preparation with a religious specialist. The quest itself typically involved going to an isolated location and engaging in prayer while forgoing food and drink for a period of up to several days. Some cultures augmented fasting and prayer with hallucinogens. In some traditions the participant would watch for an animal that behaved in a significant or unusual way. In others the participant discovered an object (often a stone) that resembled some animal. In the predominant form, the initiate had a dream (the vision) in which a spirit-being appeared. Upon receiving a sign or vision, the participant returned home and sought help in interpreting the experience. Not all vision quests were successful. Religious specialists generally advised individuals to abandon a given attempt if a vision was not received within a prescribed period of time.

The techniques of the vision quest were fundamental to every visionary experience in Native American culture, whether undertaken by ordinary people seeking contact with and advice from a guardian or by great prophets and shamans. It was not unusual for vision quests to be integral parts of more elaborate rituals such as the Sun Dance of the Plains Indians.

Despite having been heavily discouraged by Christian missionaries and even outlawed by colonial governments during the 19th and 20th centuries, vision quest participation continued as an important cultural practice for many indigenous peoples of the early 21st century.

There was a concept of soul dualism among most, if not all, Numic peoples. One soul, or soul aspect, represented vitality or life. The other represented the individual as he was in a dream or vision state. During dreams or visions, the latter soul left the body and moved in the spirit realm. At those times, the person could be subject to soul loss. At death, both souls left the body. Death rites were usually minimal. An individual was buried with his possessions, or they were destroyed. The Washoe traditionally abandoned or burned a dwelling in which a death had occurred.

FIRST CONTACT AND AFTER

Interactions with colonizers from Spain and Europe had a profound effect on Great Basin societies and cultures. Most groups from this culture area had little or no contact with Europeans or Euro-Americans until after 1800. (One exception was the Southern Ute, who had sustained contact with the Spanish in New Mexico as early as the 1600s.) Between 1810 and 1840, the fur trade brought new tools and implements to those residing in the eastern part of the region. In the 1840s, Euro-American settlement of the Great Basin began, and a surge of emigrants traveled through the area on their way to Oregon and California.

As elsewhere in the United States, government policy in the Great Basin was overtly designed to assimilate the tribes into Euro-American society. Assimilation was

Although Great Basin tribes fought to retain their traditions and their land, many native peoples of this culture area, including the Shoshone men in this picture, were eventually assimilated into Western culture. Hulton Archive/Getty Images

accomplished by undercutting the indigenous subsistence economy, removing Native American children to distant boarding schools, and suppressing native religions in favour of Christianity. Beginning in the 1840s, for instance, private-property laws favouring Euro-American mining, ranching, and farming interests either destroyed or privatized most indigenous food-gathering areas. Piñon groves were cut for firewood, fence posts, and mining timbers, and the delicate regional ecosystem was disrupted by an influx of humans and livestock.

The indigenous peoples of the Great Basin attempted to resist colonial encroachment. Mounted bands of Ute, Shoshone, Shoshone-Bannock, and Northern Paiute fought with ranchers and attacked wagon trains in attempts to drive the intruders away. The struggle culminated in several local wars and massacres in the 1850s and '6os. After 1870 the tribes were forced onto reservations or into small groups on the edges of Euro-American settlements. Their land base was reduced to a small fraction of its former size. This forced the abandonment of most aboriginal subsistence patterns in favour of agriculture and ranching, in those areas where land remained in native hands, or in wage work, usually as farmhands and ranch hands.

The Great Basin peoples were perhaps most successful in resisting religious assimilation. In 1870 and again in 1890, so-called Ghost Dance movements started among the Northern Paiute of western Nevada. The dances were millenarian, nostalgic, and peaceful in character. The 1870 movement, led by the Paiute prophet Wodziwob, centred in Nevada and California. It was an elaboration of the round dance, a traditional ceremony for the renewal and abundance of life. Wodziwob's vision indicated that the dance would resurrect the victims of an epidemic that had decimated the region a year earlier.

The 1890 movement, led by the Northern Paiute prophet Wovoka, was adopted by many tribes in the western United States. Wovoka's movement stressed peace, accommodation of Euro-American development projects, truthfulness, self-discipline, and other tenets of "right living," including performance of the round dance. His message was so apt for the time that he was soon mentoring novitiates from throughout the trans-Mississippi West. Despite Wovoka's best efforts at promoting the core aspects of the new religion, the Ghost Dance message evolved from one of renewal to one of destruction as it was taken home by novitiates from the Plains. Particularly among the many bands of Sioux, ghost dancing was thought to have the power to effect an apocalypse. If properly performed, it was believed, the tribes would have the opportunity to annihilate the colonizers (or at least drive them back to the sea), the dead would be resurrected, the bison herds would be repopulated, and traditional ways of life would be restored. Ultimately, Euro-American fears related to the movement contributed to the 1890 massacre of Lakota at Wounded Knee Creek (in present-day South Dakota). In the Great Basin, however, the movement's original message endured, and Ghost Dance congregations became important reservoirs of traditional culture that persist into the 21st century.

The 20th century fostered other religious movements in the Great Basin as well. The practice of ingesting peyote in a religious context was introduced to the Ute and Eastern Shoshone in the early 1900s by Oklahoma Indians. It later spread to other peoples in the region. Most peyote groups became part of the Native American Church, a nationally recognized religious organization. Great Basin peyote rituals are generally a mixture of aboriginal and Christian elements. Ceremonies are led by experienced individuals known as "road chiefs," since they lead believers down the peyote "road" or way. A peyote ceremony, which typically lasts all night, includes singing, praying, and ingesting those parts of the peyote cactus that produce a mild hallucinogenic experience. The tenets of the Native American Church stress moral and ethical precepts and behaviour. The Eastern Shoshone and Ute also adopted the Sun Dance from the Plains tribes. The four-day dance continues to be performed, usually annually, to ensure health for the community and valour for the participants. The Sun Dance spread to some other Great Basin groups in the second half of the 20th century. For the Ute, the Bear Dance, a spring ceremony, also remains important.

The U.S. Indian Reorganization Act (1934) led to the establishment of local elected tribal councils for the various reservations and colonies in the region. These councils have since developed a number of tribally based economic enterprises, including ranching, light industry, and tourism. They have also been plaintiffs in lawsuits seeking to reclaim ancestral lands. In 1950, for instance, the U.S. judicial system found that the Ute tribe had been illegally defrauded of land in the 19th century. While the courts did not revert title to the land, they did mandate substantial monetary compensation.

In the 1950s many tribes in the United States—including several bands of Utes and Southern Paiutes—were subject to termination, a process whereby they lost federal recognition of their Indian status and thus their eligibility for federal support of health care and other services. Although most bands fought this process, some did not regain federal status until the 1980s. Others continued to fight for recognition and land well into the early 21st century. The Western Shoshone, for instance, turned to the international court system in their efforts to regain their traditional landholdings.

Chapter 4

GREAT BASIN PEOPLES IN FOCUS

Most of the Great Basin peoples spoke Numic languages. These languages are currently divided into three groups: Western Numic, including Mono and Northern Paiute; Central Numic, including Panamint, Shoshone, and Comanche; and Southern Numic, including Kawaiisu, Ute, and Southern Paiute. Numic represents the northernmost extension of the Uto-Aztecan language family, but the precise groupings within Uto-Aztecan are not yet clear. The speakers of these languages—as well as the linguistically isolated, Hokan-speaking Washoe—are treated in the following section.

COMANCHE

In the 18th- and 19th-century, the Comanche (also erroneously called Padouca) occupied territory comprised of what is now the southern Great Plains. The name Comanche is derived from a Ute word meaning "anyone who wants to fight me all the time."

A tribe of equestrian nomads, the Comanche had previously been part of the Wyoming Shoshone. They moved south in successive stages, attacking and displacing other tribes, notably the Apache, whom they drove from the southern Plains. By the early 1800s the Comanche were very powerful, with a population estimated at 7,000 to 10,000 individuals. Their Uto-Aztecan language became a lingua franca for much of the area.

Like most other tribes of Plains Indians, the Comanche were organized into autonomous bands, local groups

COMANCHES BRAVE.

A colourized postcard featuring a Comanche warrior, posed holding a rifle and tomahawk. Loosely translated, "Comanche" means "anyone who wants to fight me all the time." Transcendental Graphics/Archive Photos/ Getty Images

formed on the basis of kinship and other social relation-ships. Buffalo products formed the core of the Comanche economy and included robes, tepee covers, sinew thread, water carriers made of the animal's stomach, and a wide variety of other goods.

The Comanche were one of the first tribes to acquire horses from the Spanish and one of the few to breed them to any extent. Highly skilled Comanche horsemen set the pattern of nomadic equestrian life that became characteristic of the Plains tribes in the 18th and 19th centuries. Comanche raids for material goods, horses, and captives carried them as far south as Durango in present-day Mexico.

In the mid-19th century the Penateka, or southern branch of the Comanche, were settled on a reserva-tion in Indian Territory (now Oklahoma). The northern segment of the tribe, however, continued the struggle to protect their realm from settlers. In 1864 Col. Christopher ("Kit") Carson led U.S. forces in an unsuc-cessful campaign against the Comanche. In 1865 the Comanche and their allies the Kiowa signed a treaty with the United States, which granted them what is now western Oklahoma, from the Red River north to the Cimarron. Upon the failure of the United States to abide by the terms of the treaty, hostilities resumed until 1867, when, in agreements made at Medicine Lodge Creek in Kansas, the Comanche, Kiowa, and Kiowa Apache undertook to settle on a reservation in Oklahoma. The government was unable to keep squatters off the land promised to the tribes, and it was after this date that some of the most violent encounters between U.S. forces and the Comanche took place.

Early 21st-century population estimates indicated some 20,000 individuals of Comanche descent.

QUANAH PARKER

(b. 1848?, near Wichita Falls, Texas, U.S.—d. Feb. 23, 1911, Cache, near Fort Sill, Okla.)

An aggressive Comanche leader and the last chief of the Kwahadi (Quahadi) band, Quanah Parker mounted an unsuccessful war (1874–75) against white encroachment in northwest Texas. He later became the main spokesman and peacetime leader of the Native Americans in the region, a role he performed for 30 years.

Comanche leader Quanah Parker (right) *and one of his wives.* Authenticated News/Archive Photos/Getty Images

Quanah was the son of Chief Peta Nocona and Cynthia Ann Parker, a white woman captured by the Comanches as a child. Quanah later added his mother's surname to his own. In 1860 Texas Rangers attacked an Indian encampment on Pease River, killing Nocona and capturing Cynthia Ann and the couple's young daughter, Prairie Flower. (Possibly hoping to protect his father's reputation, Quanah later insisted that he and Nocona were not there, but statements by eyewitnesses, including his mother, refute that assertion.) Tall and muscular, Quanah became a full warrior at age 15. A series of raids established his reputation as an aggressive and fearless fighter, and he became a war chief at a relatively young age.

Quanah moved between several Comanche bands before joining the fierce Kwahadi band—particularly bitter enemies of the buffalo hunters who had appropriated their best land on the Texas frontier and who were decimating the buffalo herds. In order to stem the onslaught of Comanche attacks on settlers and travelers, the U.S. government assigned the Indians to reservations in 1867. Quanah and his band, however, refused to cooperate and continued their raids. Attempts by the U.S. military to locate them were unsuccessful. In June 1874 Quanah and Isa-tai, a medicine man who claimed to have a potion that would protect the Indians from bullets, gathered some 250–700 warriors from among the Comanche, Cheyenne, and Kiowa and attacked about 30 white buffalo hunters quartered at Adobe Walls, Texas. Although the raid had been a failure for the Native Americans—a saloon owner had allegedly been warned of the attack—the U.S. military retaliated in force in what became known as the Red River War. Quanah's group held out on the Staked Plains for almost a year before he finally surrendered at Fort Sill.

Eventually agreeing to settle on the reservation in southwestern Oklahoma, Quanah persuaded other Comanche bands to conform. He soon became known as the principal chief of all Comanche, a position that had never existed. During the next three decades he was the main interpreter of white civilization to his people, encouraging education and agriculture, advocating on behalf of the Comanche, and becoming a success-ful businessman. Quanah also maintained elements of his own Indian culture, including polygamy, and he played a major role in creating a peyote religion that spread from the Comanche to other tribes. A national figure, he developed friendships with numerous notable men, including Pres. Theodore Roosevelt, who invited Quanah to his inauguration in 1905. Shortly there-after, Roosevelt visited Quanah at the chief's home, a 10-room residence known as Star House, in Cache, Okla.

After his death in 1911, Quanah was buried next to his mother, whose assimilation back into white civilization had been difficult. Her repeated attempts to rejoin the Comanche had been blocked by her white family, and in 1864 Prairie Flower died. Cynthia Ann reportedly starved herself to death in 1870.

MONO

The name Mono (Monachi) refers to either of two North American Indian groups, originally from what is now cen-tral California, who were related to the Northern Paiute. The Western Mono resided in the pine belt of the Sierra Nevada mountains and had a culture similar to that of the nearby Yokuts. The Owens Valley Paiute (previously called the Eastern Mono) were more similar to their neighbours from the Great Basin culture area.

Historically, the two divisions traded with each other. The Owens Valley Paiute exchanged salt, piñon nuts, bas-kets, and poison in return for acorn flour, baskets, and arrow shafts.

Traditionally, the Mono lived in small villages of as many as 50 to 75 people, organized in patrilineal families and ranging over loosely defined hunting areas. Although the power of the chief was far from absolute, his consent was required for all major religious or warlike undertakings. His greatest responsibilities were the settlement of disputes and the sanctioning of punishment.

Early 21st-century population estimates indicated some 3,000 Mono descendants.

NORTHERN PAIUTE

The Northern Paiute (or Piute; called Paviotso in Nevada) are related to the Mono of California. Like a number of other California and Southwest Indians, the Northern Paiute, who call themselves Numa, have been given the derogatory name Diggers because some of the wild foods they collected were dug from the earth. They occupied east-central California, western Nevada, and eastern Oregon. A related group, the Bannock, lived with the Shoshone in southern Idaho, where they were bison hunters. After 1840 a rush of prospectors and farmers despoiled the arid environment's meagre supply of food plants, after which the Northern Paiute acquired guns and horses and fought at intervals with the trespassers until 1874, when the last Paiute lands were appropriated by the U.S. government.

Like the Southern Paiute, the Northern Paiute were traditionally a hunting-and-gathering culture that subsisted primarily on seed, pine nuts, and small game. Families were affiliated through intermarriage, but there were no formal bands or territorial organizations except in the more fertile areas such as the Owens River Valley in California.

Population estimates in the early 21st century indicated approximately 17,000 individuals of Paiute descent.

SARAH WINNEMUCCA

(b. c. 1844, Humboldt Sink, Mex. [now in Nevada]—d. Oct. 16, 1891, Monida, Mont.)

Named Thoc-me-tony (Thocmectony, or Tocmectone, mean-ing "shell flower") at birth, Sarah Winnemucca was a Native American educator, lecturer, tribal leader, and writer best known for her book *Life Among the Piutes: Their Wrongs and Claims* (1883). Her writings, valuable for their description of Northern Paiute life and for their insights into the impact of white settlement, are among the few contemporary Native American works.

A granddaughter of Truckee and daughter of Winnemucca, both Northern Paiute chiefs, she lived during part of her child-hood in the San Joaquin Valley of California, where she learned both Spanish and English. After her return to Nevada she lived for a time with a white family and adopted the name Sarah. In 1860 she briefly attended a convent school in San Jose, Calif., until objections from the parents of white students forced her to

Paiute educator and author Sarah Winnemucca. Transcendental Graphics/Archive Photos/Getty Images

leave. During the Paiute War of 1860 and the subsequent increasingly frequent clashes between Native Americans and whites, she suffered the loss of several family members. She attempted the role of peacemaker on a few occasions and from 1868 to 1871 served as an interpreter at Camp McDermitt in northeastern Nevada. In 1872 she accompanied her tribe to a new reservation, the Malheur, in southeastern Oregon.

Winnemucca for a time was an interpreter for the reservation agent, but the appointment of a new and unsympathetic agent in 1876 ended her service as well as a period of relative quiet on the reservation. On the outbreak of the Bannock War in 1878, she learned that her father and others had been taken hostage and offered to help the army scout the Bannock territory. Covering more than 100 miles (161 km) of trail through Idaho and Oregon, Winnemucca located the Bannock camp, spirited her father and many of his companions away, and returned with valuable intelligence for General O.O. Howard. She was scout, aide, and interpreter to Howard during the resulting campaign against the Bannocks.

After a year of teaching in a school for Native American children at Vancouver Barracks, Washington Territory, and her marriage late in 1881 to L.H. Hopkins, an army officer, Winnemucca, often known among whites as "the Princess," went on an eastern lecture tour to arouse public opinion. With the help of General Howard, Elizabeth Peabody, and others, the tour was a success, and sales of her *Life Among the Piutes* were brisk. Her several attempts to secure a promised allotment of reservation lands to individual Paiutes came to nothing.

SHOSHONE

The Shoshone occupied territory from what is now southeastern California across central and eastern Nevada and northwestern Utah into southern Idaho and western Wyoming. The Shoshone of historic times were organized into four groups: Western, or unmounted, Shoshone, centred in Nevada; Northern, or horse, Shoshone of northern Utah and Idaho; Wind River Shoshone in western Wyoming; and Comanche in western Texas, a comparatively recent offshoot of the Wind River group.

Painting on a moose hide depicting a buffalo hunt. In the centre, a group of Shoshone perform a native Sun Dance. ©Universal Images Group/ SuperStock

The Western Shoshone were organized into loosely affiliated family bands that subsisted on wild plants, small mammals, fish, and insects. Each family was independently nomadic during most of the year and joined other families only briefly for activities such as rabbit drives, antelope hunts, or dancing. Like other Great Basin Indians, they were sometimes referred to by the derogatory name Diggers because of their practice of digging tubers and roots for food. A few Western Shoshone obtained horses after the colonial settlement of Nevada and Utah.

The Wind River Shoshone and Northern Shoshone probably acquired horses as early as 1680, before Spanish occupation of their lands. They formed loosely organized bands of mounted buffalo hunters and warriors and adopted many Plains Indian cultural traits such as the use of tepees and the importance of counting coup (striking or touching an enemy in warfare in a prescribed way) as a war honour. Sacagawea, who acted as interpreter and guide for the Lewis and Clark expedition of 1804–06, is thought to have been a member of either the Wind River or the Northern group.

SACAGAWEA

(b. c. 1788, near the Continental Divide at the present-day Idaho-Montana border—d. Dec. 20, 1812?, Fort Manuel, on the Missouri River, Dakota Territory)

Serving as an interpreter, the Shoshone woman Sacagawea traveled thousands of wilderness miles with the Lewis and Clark Expedition (1804–06), from the Mandan-Hidatsa villages in the Dakotas to the Pacific Northwest.

It is difficult to separate fact from legend in Sacagawea's life. Historians disagree on the dates of her birth and death and even on her name. In Hidatsa, Sacagawea (pronounced with a hard *g*) translates into "Bird Woman." Alternatively, Sacajawea means "Boat Launcher" in Shoshone. Still others favour the spelling Sakakawea. The Lewis and Clark journals generally support the Hidatsa derivation.

Statue erected in Montana honouring Native American guide Sacagawea. Marilyn Angel Wynn/Nativestock.com/Collection Mix: Subjects/Getty Images

A Lemhi Shoshone woman, she was about 12 years old when a Hidatsa raiding party captured her near the Missouri River's headwaters about 1800. Enslaved and taken to their Knife River earth-lodge villages near present-day Bismarck, N.D., she was purchased by French Canadian fur trader Toussaint Charbonneau and became one of his plural wives about 1804. They resided in Metaharta, one of the Hidatsa villages.

When explorers Meriwether Lewis and William Clark arrived at the Mandan-Hidatsa villages and built Fort Mandan to spend the winter of 1804–05, they hired Charbonneau as an interpreter to accompany them to the Pacific Ocean. Because he did not speak Sacagawea's language and because the expedition party needed to communicate with the Shoshones to acquire horses to cross the mountains, the explorers agreed that the pregnant Sacagawea should also accompany them. On Feb. 11, 1805, she gave birth to a son, Jean Baptiste.

Departing on April 7, the expedition ascended the Missouri. Sacagawea proved to be a significant asset in numerous ways: searching for edible plants, making moccasins and clothing, as well as allaying suspicions of approaching Indian tribes through her presence. A woman and child accompanying a party of men indicated peaceful intentions.

By mid-August the expedition encountered a band of Shoshones led by Sacagawea's brother Cameahwait. The reunion of sister and brother had a positive effect on Lewis and Clark's negotiations for the horses and guide that enabled them to cross the Rocky Mountains.

After the expedition's return to the Mandan-Hidatsa villages, the Charbonneau family disengaged from the expedition party. Charbonneau eventually received $409.16 and 320 acres (130 hectares) for his services. Clark wanted to do more for their family, so he offered to assist them and eventually secured Charbonneau a position as an interpreter. The family traveled to St. Louis in 1809 to baptize their son and left him in the care of Clark, who had earlier offered to provide him with an education. Shortly after the birth of a daughter named Lisette, a woman identified only as Charbonneau's wife (but believed to be Sacagawea) died at the end of 1812 at Fort Manuel, near present-day Mobridge, S.D. Clark became the legal guardian of Lisette and Jean Baptiste and listed Sacagawea as deceased in a list he compiled in the 1820s. Some biographers and oral traditions contend that it was another of Charbonneau's wives who died in 1812 and that Sacagawea went to live among the Comanches, started another family, rejoined the Shoshones, and died on Wyoming's Wind River Reservation on April 9, 1884. These accounts can likely be attributed to other Shoshone women whose experiences were similar to those of Sacagawea.

After acquiring horses, the Comanche split off from the Wind River Shoshone and moved south into Texas. Comanche bands were feared by the Spaniards of the Southwest because they subsisted as much by plunder as by buffalo hunting.

Early 21st-century population estimates indicated some 41,000 descendants of the four Shoshone groups.

SOUTHERN PAIUTE

The Southern Paiute, who speak Ute, at one time occupied what are now southern Utah, northwestern Arizona, southern Nevada, and southeastern California, the latter group being known as the Chemehuevi. Although encroached upon and directed into reservations by the U.S. government in the 19th century, the Southern Paiute had comparatively little friction with settlers and the U.S. military. Many found ways to stay on their traditional lands, usually by working on ranches or living on the fringes of the new towns.

Like the Northern Paiute, the Southern Paiute were a hunting-and-gathering culture that subsisted primarily on seed, pine nuts, and small game, although many Southern Paiute also planted small gardens. Because of the warm climate, they required only minimal shelter and little clothing except rabbit-skin blankets. They made a variety of baskets for gathering and cooking food.

Population estimates in the early 21st century indicated approximately 17,000 individuals of Paiute descent.

WASHOE

The Washoe of the Great Basin region made their home around Lake Tahoe in what is now California. Their peak numerical strength before contact with settlers may have been 1,500.

Traditionally, the Washoe were fishers, hunters of small mammals, and gatherers of pine nuts, acorns, and various roots and berries. They depended on deer and antelope for food, for clothing, and for hides to cover their cone-shaped dwellings. They were especially noted for their superb basketry.

The basic, traditional socioeconomic unit of the Washoe was the extended family. During winter this group would reside together. The able-bodied members migrated each summer into the eastern valleys in search of roots, berries, and small game. Goods and services were distributed in various ways: through familial sharing, in gift and ceremonial exchange at feasts for motives of prestige and good relations, and in ritual gift giving at important stages of the life cycle.

Shamanism was an important part of traditional Washoe life. A shaman, or medicine man or woman, was believed to be able to cause and cure disease. Complex rituals celebrating important stages of the life cycle were also recounted.

Some 2,000 Washoe descendants were reported in 21st-century population estimates.

SOUTHWEST INDIANS

More than 20 percent of Native Americans in the United States live in the southwestern United States, principally in the present-day states of Arizona and New Mexico. The Southwest culture area is located between the Rocky Mountains and the Mexican Sierra Madre. The Continental Divide separates the landscape into the watersheds of two great river systems: the Colorado–Gila–San Juan, in the west, and the Rio Grande–Pecos, in the east. The environment is arid, with some areas averaging less than 4 inches (10 cm) of precipitation each year. Droughts are common. Despite its low moisture content, coarse texture, and occasional salty patches, the soil of most of the Southwest is relatively fertile.

The distribution of resources in the region is determined more by elevation than by latitude. The predominant landscape feature in the north is the Colorado Plateau, a cool, arid plain into which the Colorado and Rio Grande systems have carved deep canyons. Precipitation tends to be greater at the plateau's higher elevations, which support scrub and piñon-juniper woodland, rattlesnakes, rabbits, coyotes, bobcats, and mule deer. At lower elevations the plateau also supports grasses and antelope. To the south the river systems descend from the plateau, and canyons, mesas, and steep escarpments give way to a basin and range system. River valleys here support clusters of cottonwood, willow, mesquite, and sycamore trees, and mule deer, fish, and waterfowl. The areas away from the rivers are characterized by desert flora and fauna, including mesquite, creosote bush, cactus, yucca, small mammals, and reptiles.

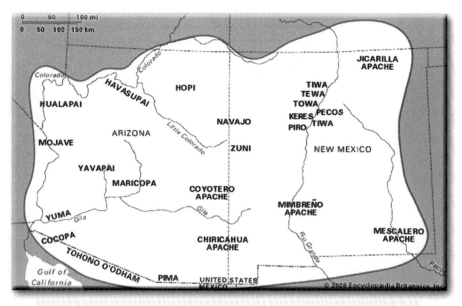

Distribution of Southwest Indians and their reservations and lands.

CULTURAL CHARACTERISTICS

The people of the Southwest were preceded in the region by Cochise culture, a desert-adapted hunting-and-gathering culture whose diet emphasized plant foods and small game. This group lived in the region as early as *c.* 7000 BCE.

Farming became important for subsequent residents including the Ancestral Pueblo (Anasazi; *c.* 100–1600 CE), the Mogollon (*c.* 200–1450 CE), and the Hohokam (*c.* 200–1400 CE). These groups lived in permanent and semipermanent settlements that they sometimes built near (or even on) sheltering cliffs; developed various forms of irrigation; grew crops of maize (corn), beans, and squash; and had complex social and ritual habits. It is believed that the Ancestral Pueblo were the ancestors of the modern Pueblo Indians, that the Hohokam were the ancestors of the Pima and Tohono O'odham

The Cliff Palace, which has 150 rooms, 23 kivas, and several towers, at Mesa Verde National Park in Colorado. © C. McIntyre—PhotoLink/ Getty Images

(Papago), and that the Mogollon dispersed or joined other communities.

LANGUAGE

Despite many other cultural commonalities, the Southwest was home to representatives from several North American Indian language families, including Hokan, Uto-Aztecan, Tanoan, Keresan, Kiowa-Tanoan, Penutian, and Athabaskan.

The Hokan-speaking Yuman peoples were the westernmost residents of the region. They lived in the river valleys and the higher elevations of the basin and range system there. The cultures of the so-called River

Yumans—including the Quechan (Yuma), Mojave, Cocopa, and Maricopa, who resided on the Lower Colorado and the Gila rivers—combined some traditions of the Southwest culture area with others of the California Indians. The Upland Yumans, including the Havasupai, Hualapai, and Yavapai, lived on secondary and ephemeral streams in the western basins and ranges.

Two groups that spoke Uto-Aztecan languages resided in the southwestern portion of the culture area, near the border between the present-day states of Arizona (U.S.) and Sonora (Mex.). The Tohono O'odham (Papago) were located west of the Santa Cruz River. The closely related Pima lived along the middle Gila River.

The Pueblo Indians were linguistically diverse. Those living along the Rio Grande and its tributaries are generally referred to as the eastern Pueblos, while those on the Colorado Plateau are assigned to the western division. The eastern group included the Keresan-speaking Zia, Santa Ana, San Felipe, Santo Domingo, and Cochiti, and representatives of three members of the Kiowa-Tanoan language family: the Tewa-speaking San Ildefonso, San Juan, Santa Clara, Tesuque, and Nambe; the Tiwa-speaking Isleta, Sandia, Taos, and Picurís; and the Towa-speaking Jemez. The western Pueblo tribes included the Hopi (Uto-Aztecan), Hano (Tanoan), Zuni (Penutian), and Acoma and Laguna (Keresan).

The Navajo and the closely related Apache spoke Athabaskan languages. The Navajo lived on the Colorado Plateau near the Hopi villages. The Apache traditionally resided in the range and basin systems south of the plateau. The major Apache tribes included the Western Apache, Chiricahua, Mescalero, Jicarilla, Lipan, and Kiowa Apache. The Athabaskan-speaking groups migrated from northwestern North America to the Southwest and probably did not reach the area until sometime between 1100 and 1500 CE.

FOOD PRODUCTION AND SOCIAL STRUCTURE

Both farming and hunting and gathering were important economic strategies in the Southwest. Proximity to water was the main determinant of the degree to which a given culture relied upon domesticated or wild foods. A number of domesticated resources were more or less ubiquitous throughout the culture area, including maize (corn), beans, squash, cotton, turkeys, and dogs. During the period of Spanish colonization, horses, burros, and sheep were added to the agricultural repertoire, as were new varieties of beans, plus wheat, melons, apricots, peaches, and other cultigens.

Most groups coped with the desert environment by occupying sites on waterways. These ranged in quality and reliability from large permanent rivers such as the Colorado, through secondary streams, to washes or gullies that channeled seasonal rainfall but were dry most of the year. Precipitation was unpredictable and fell in just a few major rains each year, compelling many groups to engage in irrigation. While settlements along major waterways could rely almost entirely on agriculture for food, groups whose access was limited to ephemeral waterways typically used farming to supplement hunting and gathering, relying on wild foods during much of the year.

In some other cultural traits, such as kinship and economic strategies, the Southwest Indians fall into subgroups that are distinguishable within the cultural area, but larger than the tribal unit. These are discussed within the "Southwest peoples in Focus" in the following chapter.

PUEBLO ARCHITECTURE

The traditional architecture of the Pueblo Indians consists of multistoried, permanent, attached homes modeled after the cliff dwellings built by the Ancestral Pueblo (Anasazi) culture beginning in approximately 1150 CE. This architectural form continued to be used by many Pueblo peoples in the early 21st century.

Traditional pueblo construction used limestone blocks or large adobe bricks. The latter were made from clay and water, and generally measured approximately 8 by 16 inches (20 by 40 cm), with a thickness of 4 to 6 inches (10 to 15 cm). In the early 21st century, modern construction materials were sometimes used in tandem with adobe, creating stronger and more durable structures.

In a typical pueblo building, adobe blocks form the walls of each room as well as a central courtyard. Buildings can be up to five stories tall. Usually each floor is set back from the floor below so that a given building resembles a stepped pyramid. This architectural form enables the roof of each level to serve as a terrace for the level above. Movement between levels was traditionally accomplished by means of wooden ladders, although staircases are now used as well. Ground floor rooms had (and in some cases, continue to have) no ground-level doors. Used almost exclusively for storage, primarily of grain, they were traditionally entered through rooftop openings. Most rooms above the ground floor can be entered by doorways from adjoining rooms.

Most pueblo residential groups comprise nuclear or extended families. Numerous families may live in a given building. Families typically have several connecting rooms, which are often arranged in a line radiating out from the central plaza of the pueblo. Additions to a family's section of the pueblo are generally added above or behind the original rooms. Traditionally each pueblo also had two or more kivas, or ceremonial rooms.

FAMILY AND EDUCATION

The rearing of children was taken to be a serious responsibility by all of the Southwestern tribes. Most felt that adults were obliged to engage in frequent self-reflection and redirection to remain members of the tribes and consequently that each child had to learn how to be the sort of adult who took seriously membership in the tribe. In other words, ethnic identity was something to be achieved rather than assumed.

Children were generally treated with warmth and permissiveness until they were weaned, a period that might last from one to three or four years. Care was taken not to agitate a child unduly: young children nursed on demand, and weaning and toilet training were gradual. Children were protected from harm through careful tending and by means of magical prophylactics. Cradles and cradleboards were used, especially during the first year of life. The Hopi viewed swaddling as the first of many periods of conditioning that helped the individual to gain self-control. From birth, children were treated as an integral part of the family. Among the Navajo, for instance, the cradleboard was hung on a wall or pillar so that the child would be at eye level with others seated in the family circle.

From the beginning of childhood there was training in customary gender roles. Little girls began to learn food processing and childcare, and little boys were given chores such as collecting firewood or tending animals. However, the most important work of childhood was the internalization of the abiding precept that individuals were expected to pull their own weight, at every age grade, according to their gender, strength, and talent.

When they were between five and seven years old, boys began to associate almost exclusively with the men

Mizheh and Babe, *portrait of an Apache woman holding a child in a cradleboard, photograph by Edward S. Curtis,* c. *1906.* Library of Congress, Washington, D.C. (neg. no. LC-USZ62-46949)

of their households, who from then on directed their education into masculine tasks and lore. At about the same age, girls began to take on increasing responsibility for the exacting tasks of the household. Among the more nomadic groups, particularly the Apacheans, the physical strength, stoicism, and skill needed for battle were stressed, and training in the arts of war intensified as a youth grew to young manhood. Even among the more pacifist Pueblos, however, boys learned agility, endurance, and speed in running. Racing was important to the Pueblos because it was considered to possess magical efficacy in helping plants, animals, and human beings to grow.

KACHINAS

In traditional religions of the Pueblo Indians of North America, kachinas (*katsinas*) are divine and ancestral spirit beings who interact with humans. Each Pueblo culture has distinct forms and variations of kachinas, and there are more than 500 such beings.

Kachinas are believed to reside with the tribe for half of each year. They will allow themselves to be seen by a community if its men properly perform a traditional ritual while wearing kachina masks and other regalia. The spirit-being depicted on the mask is thought to be actually present with or within the performer, temporarily transforming him.

Kachinas are also depicted in small, heavily ornamented carved-wood dolls, which are traditionally made by the men of a tribe and presented to girls. Boys receive bows and arrows. These wooden dolls are used to teach the identities of the kachinas and the symbolism of their regalia. The identity of the spirit is depicted not by the form of the doll's body, which is usually simple and flat, but primarily by the applied colour and elaborate feather, leather, and, occasionally, fabric ornamentation of its mask.

Despite these similarities, tribes did show some marked differences in their child-rearing practices. The children of the Tohono O'odham and Pima were probably allowed the greatest freedom of action. Nevertheless they were expected to recognize seniority and show respect for age, regardless of sex; to promote group solidarity; and to respect the role, function, and opinion of every member of the band. Children were expected to make age-appropriate progress in these areas and in contributing to the group's subsistence.

In contrast, Pueblo children were subjected to extremes of control. These tribes stressed life-crisis ceremonies that offered symbolic resolution to the major problems faced by the community. Children who failed to reach certain (usually behavioral) benchmarks in a timely manner were pushed in prescribed ways to meet the standard. For example, all Hopi children participated in the kachina ceremony at about seven years of age. Its purpose was to initiate them into the tribe and to facilitate their introduction to religious practice. During the ceremony, it is reported that all the children were ritually whipped to exorcise evil influences, but those children who frequently misbehaved or showed a lack of self-control were whipped more severely than the others.

RELIGIOUS BELIEFS AND PRACTICES

Like most Native American religions, those of the Southwest Indians were generally characterized by animism and shamanism. Animists perceive the world as filled with living entities: spirit-beings that animate the sun, moon, rain, thunder, animals, plants, topographic features, and many other natural phenomena. Shamans are individuals who have achieved a level of knowledge or power regarding physiological and spiritual health, especially its maintenance, recovery, or destruction. Always in a somewhat liminal state, shamans had to be acutely aware of the community's goings-on or risk the consequences: a number of 19th-century accounts report the execution of Pima shamans who were believed to have caused people to sicken and die.

The spectacular, communally centred Pueblo ceremonies for rain and growth reflected a conception of the universe in which every person, animal, plant, and supernatural being was considered significant. Without the active participation of every individual in the group, it was believed that the life-giving sun would not return from his "winter house" after the solstice, the rain would not fall, and the crops would not grow. In fact, Pueblo groups generally believed that the cosmic order was in perpetual danger of breaking down and that an annual cycle of ceremonies was a crucial factor in the continued existence of the world.

In the Pueblo view, humans affected the world through their actions, emotions, and attitudes, among other things, and each year kachinas visited communities that fostered metaphysical harmony. The number and form of the kachinas varied from one community to the next and reflected the concerns and consequences of life in a desert environment. Many of the hundreds of kachinas known to scholars were spirits of corn, squash, and rain. There were also kachinas of tricksters, ogres, hunters, and many animals. Each individual kachina had a distinctive appearance, and during annual rituals they were thought to possess or share the bodies of dancers whose regalia matched that appearance. The kachina religion was most active among the western Pueblos and was less important as one traveled east.

The Apache conceived of the universe as inhabited by a great variety of powerful entities, including animals, plants, witches (evil shamans), superhuman beings, rocks, and mountains. Each could exert force in the world for good or ill and required individual propitiation. Each was personalized, talked to, sung to, scolded, or praised. Apache ceremonies were concerned mainly with the magical coercion of these powerful entities for the curing of disease and the acquisition of personal success in hunting and warfare.

Navajo ceremonies were based on an elaboration of a similarly animistic view of the universe, with the power sources both diffuse and specific. Power was localized in a great many autonomous beings who were dangerous and unpredictable. These were of two classes: Earth Surface People (human beings, ghosts, and witches) and Holy People (supernaturals who could aid or harm Earth Surface People

BLESSINGWAY

The Blessingway is the central ceremony of a complex system of Navajo healing ceremonies known as sings, or chants, that are designed to restore equilibrium to the cosmos. Anthropologists have grouped these ceremonies into six major divisions: the Blessingways, Holyways, Lifeways, Evilways, War Ceremonials, and Gameways.

Parts of the general Blessingway, especially the songs, are included in most Navajo ceremonies. Unlike the other healing ceremonies, the Blessingways are not intended to cure illness but are used to invoke positive blessings and to avert misfortune. The Blessingway is comparatively short, lasting only two nights, and is often part of longer rites. Among other things, it is performed to bless and protect the home, to prevent complications of pregnancy, and to enhance the good fortune that attendees and participants hope to foster through the *kinaalda* (girl's puberty rites). As a part of Navajo religious practices, the Blessingway is considered to be a highly spiritual, sacred, and private event.

by sending sickness). As they turned away from hunting and raiding in favour of agriculture and herding, the Navajo focused their attention on elaborate rituals or "sings" that aimed to cure sickness and bring an individual into harmony with his family group, nature, and the supernatural.

In contrast to the animistic religions of other Southwest tribes, the River Yumans believed that a single animating principle or deity was the source of all supernatural power. There was only one medium, dreaming, for acquiring the supernatural protection, guidance, and power that were considered necessary for success in life. Sequences of traditional myths acquired through dreaming were converted into songs and acted out in ceremonies. The pursuit of such power sometimes caused an individual religious or war leader to abandon all other activities—farming, food collecting, and even hunting. It seems to have been no coincidence that this form of spiritual quest occurred only where one could count on regular and plentiful crops.

The religion of the Tohono O'odham seems to reflect their position between the River Yumans and the Pueblos. Not only did they "sing for power" and go on individual vision quests like the former, but they also held regular communal ceremonies to keep the world in order.

COLONIZATION AND CHANGE

The indigenous peoples of the Southwest culture area attempted to maintain a delicate balance between population and natural resources. If the population outgrew available resources, a segment of the group might split off and move to a habitat resembling that of its parent group. Under normal conditions the new colony was so constituted to reproduce as far as possible the parent culture even in its most esoteric aspects. If prolonged drought occurred, an entire community might migrate. Alternatively human pressures from without, such as raids by marauding bands or aggressive missionization, could cause a tribe to consolidate and move to more easily defended sites. In the 1700s, for instance, Tohono O'odham settlements consolidated into large compact villages for defense against the Apache.

RESISTANCE TO COLONIZATION

Spain hoped to gain gold, slaves, and converts to Roman Catholicism from its New World colonies. Soldiers and missionaries who undertook the work of conquest were promised a portion of those riches. Not surprisingly, rumours of golden cities soon abounded, though of course none were actually discovered. In 1536 the Spanish explorer Álvar Núñez Cabeza de Vaca recounted stories of golden cities rumoured to be somewhere in the North American interior. His report spurred the government to sponsor an exploratory trip by the friar Marcos de Niza (1539), who reported seeing from afar cities of vast riches. These were probably the Zuni pueblos and the friar's mistake is understandable given that the Zuni towns were larger than many of the Spanish outposts in Mexico.

Francisco Vázquez de Coronado subsequently led an expedition (1540–42) that included some 300 soldiers, several missionaries, approximately 1,000 indigenous labourers, and some 1,000 pack animals. Overwintering on the Rio Grande, Coronado demanded provisions from nearby pueblos. His men also molested several Pueblo women. Indigenous resistance was met with force: the Spanish executed some 200 Pueblo individuals, many through burning at the stake. Spain was in the throes of the Inquisition during this period, the methods of which had been quickly transferred to the Americas. The surviving Pueblos in the area were horrified and they fled.

Permanent colonial occupation of the Southwest was initiated in 1598 under the leadership of Juan de Oñate, who had been commissioned to found a series of Spanish towns in the region. When Oñate's troops met with resistance at Acoma pueblo in 1599, they killed perhaps 800 of the town's 6,000 residents. The 80 surviving men of Acoma were punished by the amputation of a foot, the women and adolescents were sentenced to 20 years of slavery, and children under age 12 were given to the missions.

The next eight decades saw the spread of Catholicism and the establishment of the *encomienda*, a system of tribute paid through indigenous labour and foodstuffs. Although these changes were burdensome, the penalties the Pueblos felt for engaging in traditional religious activities such as kachina dances were far worse. These rituals were seen by the Catholic priests as abominations, and, in order to stamp out traditional religion, the missionaries destroyed regalia and punished religious leaders severely. Reports of tortures such as flaying and dismemberment are common during this period.

By about 1670 it had become increasingly clear to the Pueblos that the world was sliding into chaos. In addition to deaths from torture and execution, many Pueblos died during recurrent epidemics of smallpox and other Old World diseases to which they had little resistance. Further, the Apachean tribes had begun to raid freely. Raids combined with a series of devastating droughts and the *encomienda* to cause mass starvation in the pueblos. Given their worldview, the Pueblo peoples thought it imperative to reestablish their religious observances. In 1680 they effected an organized revolt against the Spanish, killing nearly all the Catholic priests and driving the conquerors out of the region.

METHODS OF CULTURAL PRESERVATION

For 12 years after the Pueblo Rebellion, the Pueblos were free from foreign rule, but this circumstance was soon reversed. The returning soldiers and missionaries employed a divide-and-conquer strategy, overcoming each pueblo individually. By 1696 Spanish rule again prevailed in the Southwest. Having had a bit more than a decade in which to reorganize and reevaluate their position vis-à-vis the colonizers, the Pueblos appeared to accede to missionization. They did not, however, abandon their traditional religious and cultural practices. Instead, they took such practices underground and thus preserved many aspects of their pre-Columbian cultural traditions.

With differing levels of exposure to colonial conquest, it is to be expected that the traditions of the eastern and western Pueblos were differentially preserved. Unless totally destroyed, the western Pueblos did not surrender structurally to foreign control. Social organization among these groups was characterized by robust and cross-cutting levels of clan and secret society memberships. These were rather easily disguised and the people were thus able to resist (or only superficially absorb) externally imposed social change.

In contrast, the eastern Pueblos had more central-ized forms of social organization based on moieties. The moieties, in turn, were the foundation of both civil and spiritual life. When combined with the greater levels of subjugation to which these groups were exposed, the moiety systems proved vulnerable to attack at both the sociopolitical and the ceremonial levels. Most of the east-ern Pueblos incorporated at least some aspects of the Spanish system into their own structures, creating a syn-cretic blend of the two. The Tohono O'odham produced their own Christian sect, a blend of native and mission practices known as Sonoran Catholicism.

During the 16th, 17th, and 18th centuries, the Apachean tribes fought the foreign control of the Spanish and attempted to gain and hold territory surrounding the Pueblo communities. They also took note of the material conditions of these groups—indigenous and Spanish—and selectively incorporated such things as horses, sheep, cattle, woven goods, and dry land agricultural techniques. While fiercely preserving their unique tribal identities, the Apacheans also engaged in a long period of cultural acquisition and remodeling.

In the 19th century, a period of relative peace for the Pueblo groups, the Apachean peoples encountered con-siderable difficulty. During this period the Southwest was ceded by Spain to Mexico (1821) and later became part of the United States (1848). Although the American Civil

War slowed U.S. colonization of the region, Apachean actions against settlers were reported in newspapers and caused great public outcry. In 1863, Kit Carson was ordered to pacify the Navajo and led U.S. Army forces in the systematic destruction of the tribe's fields and livestock. Carson's forces captured some 8,000 Navajo who subsequently endured the "Long Walk" from their homeland near Canyon de Chelly in northeastern Arizona to Fort Sumner, N.M., some 300 miles (483 km) away. They were interred at the nearby Bosque Redondo camp from 1864 to 1868. After their release, the Navajo returned to their communities and began the rebuilding process.

The Apache were more difficult to conquer, particularly as several incidents of treachery, rape, and murder by members of the U.S. military instigated extreme wariness on the part of these tribes. Military pressure did cause some of the more sedentary Apache bands to move to reservations following the Civil War, but many did not trust promises of peace and chose to flee to the canyon country of the Colorado Plateau or southward, to Mexico. Although most were captured and removed to reservations by 1875, others, led by luminaries including Geronimo, continued to engage in spirited resistance until their final capture in 1886. Those who had continued armed resistance were transported to Florida, and later to Alabama, only returning to the Southwest in 1894. Geronimo, however, was seen as a figurehead of resistance and so was not allowed to return. He died in custody in 1909.

DEVELOPMENTS IN THE 20TH AND 21ST CENTURIES

The processes of change accelerated at the end of the 19th century and the beginning of the 20th. The isolation of the region had combined with its arid climate and the fierce resistance of the Apacheans to slow Euro-American settlement and urbanization. At the same time military defeat, the loss of traditional lands, and missionary efforts to change their religious beliefs and practices had fostered among many tribes a sense of rejection and bitterness against colonizers.

U.S. policies toward indigenous peoples in most of the 20th century were disparate and often unevenly applied, but shared the common goal of assimilation. In the first half of the century tribal governments were developed and empowered with legal authority. A variety of rural development projects also took place, including rural electrification and the building of schools, hospitals, irrigation systems, highways, and telephone lines. The 1950s, '60s, and '70s saw the advancement of a policy called termination, in which many tribes lost their status as sovereign entities. By the late 20th century some "terminated" Southwestern groups had filed petitions to regain federal status.

Despite rural development and other projects, reservation life remained generally difficult when compared to that of the rest of the American population, especially among the Tohono O'odham, Hopi, Fort Apache, and some of the highland Yuman tribes. Farming and sheep operations remained economic mainstays in much of the region. The reassignment of a substantial portion of Hopi common lands to the Navajo, an action that the Hopi claim abrogated federal treaties, contributed to Hopi impoverishment. Although the federal

Herding Sheep, *watercolour on paper by Allan Houser, a Chiricahua Apache, 1953; in the Denver Art Museum.* Courtesy of the Denver Art Museum, Colorado

judiciary ruled the taking was legal and the U.S. Congress in 1996 passed legislation it hoped would resolve the dispute, the reassignment remained a point of contention into the 21st century.

By the early 21st century the tribes of the Southwest had formed a variety of business development units, tribally owned enterprises, and other economic ventures. Many had developed tourism programs. These in turn provided jobs and a venue for the sale of indigenous arts such as jewelry, pottery, and textiles. Some tribes chose to allow the development of their rich mineral resources, principally coal and uranium, under closely monitored conditions. However, the ecological and spiritual costs of large mining operations made many skeptical of this form of development.

Chapter 6

SOUTHWEST PEOPLES IN FOCUS

The diversity of the peoples of the Southwest is reflected in their differing economic strategies and the great variety of languages spoken. Three distinguishable subgroups were predominant within this culture area: the collective Yumans, Pima, and Tohono O'odham; the Pueblo; and the Apacheans, particularly the Apache and the Navajo.

YUMANS, PIMA, AND TOHONO O'ODHAM

The western and southern reaches of the culture area were home to the Yuman groups and the Pima and Tohono O'odham (Papago). These peoples shared a number of cultural features, principally in terms of kinship and social organization, although their specific subsistence strategies represented a continuum from full-time agriculture to full-time foraging.

Kinship was usually reckoned bilaterally, through both the male and female lines. For those groups that raised crops, the male line was somewhat privileged as fields were commonly passed from father to son. Most couples chose to reside near the husband's family (patrilocality), and clan membership was patrilineal. In general women were responsible for most domestic tasks, such as food preparation and child-rearing, while male tasks included the clearing of fields and hunting.

The most important social unit for all these groups was the extended family, related individuals who lived and

93

worked together. Groups of families living in a given locale formed bands. Typically the male head of each family participated in an informal band council that settled disputes (often over land ownership, among the farming groups) and made decisions regarding community problems. Band leadership accrued to those with proven skills in activities such as farming, hunting, and consensus-building. A number of bands constituted the tribe. Except for the Pima, tribes were usually organized quite loosely but were politically important as the unit that determined whether relations with neighbouring groups were harmonious or not. Among the Yumans, the tribe provided the people with a strong ethnic identity, although in other cases most individuals identified more strongly with a smaller unit, such as the family or band.

The most desirable bottomlands along the Colorado and Gila rivers were densely settled by the so-called River Yumans, including the Mojave, Quechan, Cocopa, and Maricopa. They lived in riverside hamlets and their dwellings included houses made of log frameworks covered with sand, brush, or wattle-and-daub. The rivers provided plentiful water despite a minimum of rainfall and the hot desert climate. Overflowing their banks each spring, they provided fresh silt and moisture to small, irregular fields where people cultivated several varieties of maize (corn) as well as beans, pumpkins, melons, and grasses. Abundant harvests were supplemented with wild fruits and seeds, fish, and small game.

The Upland Yumans (including the Hualapai, Havasupai, and Yavapai), the Pima, and the Tohono O'odham lived on the Gila and Salt rivers, along smaller streams, and along seasonal waterways. The degree to which they relied upon agriculture depended upon their distance from permanently flowing water. Those who lived near such waterways built stone canals with which they irrigated fields of corn, beans, and squash. Those with no permanently flowing water planted crops in the alluvial fans at the mouths of washes and built low walls or check dams to slow the torrents caused by brief but intense summer rains. These latter groups relied more extensively on wild foods than on agriculture. Some engaged in no agriculture whatsoever, instead living in a fashion similar to the Great Basin Indians.

Upland settlement patterns also reflected differential access to water. Hamlets near permanent streams were occupied all year and included dome-shaped houses with walls and roofs of wattle-and-daub or thatch. The groups that relied on ephemeral streams divided their time between summer settlements near their crops and dry-season camps at higher elevations where fresh water and game were more readily available. Summer residences were usually dome-shaped and built of thatch, while lean-tos and windbreaks served as shelter during the rest of the year.

YUMANS (HOKAN SPEAKERS)

The Hokan group of American Indian languages includes 14 families of North American Indian languages once spoken in the southwestern United States from northern California to southern Texas and in northern Mexico.

As mentioned in a previous chapter, the Hokan language is notable for its frequent use of affixes (such as prefixes and suffixes) and compound words to form unusually long words. The Yana language is also of interest because it has two "dialects," one used exclusively by males to males and the other used in speech to or by females. The Mojave and the Quechan are two of the best-known speakers of Hokan languages. (The Yana, also Hokan speakers, are treated with the California Indians.)

MOJAVE

The Mojave (Mohave) were farmers of the Mojave Desert who traditionally resided along the lower Colorado River in what are now the U.S. states of Arizona and California and in northern Mexico. This river valley was a patch of green surrounded by barren desert and was subject to an annual flood that left a large deposit of fertile silt. Traditionally, planting began as soon as the floodwaters receded. Unlike some of the desert farmers to the east, whose agricultural endeavours were surrounded by considerable ritual intended to ensure success, the Mojave almost totally ignored rituals associated with crops. In addition to farming, the Mojave engaged in considerable fishing, hunting, and gathering of wild plants.

Hamlets were built wherever there was suitable land for farming, and the fields were owned by the people who cleared them. Formal government among the Mojave consisted mainly of a hereditary tribal chief who functioned as a leader and adviser. Although they did not live in concentrated settlements, the Mojave possessed a strong national identity that became most evident in times of war. As male prestige was based on success and bravery in battle, all able-bodied men generally took part in military activities, which were typically led by a single war chief. The usual enemies of the Mojave were other riverine Yuman peoples, except for the Yuma proper, who were their trusted allies during conflicts. Each combatant generally specialized in or was assigned a single kind of weaponry. Battles included archers, clubbers, and stick men and were often highly stylized.

In religion the Mojave believed in a supreme creator and attached great significance to dreams, which were considered the source of special powers. Public ceremonies included the singing of cycles of dreamed songs that recited myths. Usually the narrative retold a mythic or legendary journey, and some cycles consisted of hundreds of songs.

Population estimates indicated approximately 2,000 Mojave descendants in the early 21st century.

Quechan

The Quechan, who are sometimes considered California Indians, are people of the fertile Colorado River Valley who shared many traditions of the Southwest Indians. Despite low precipitation and a desert climate, the river provided abundant water, flooding each spring and providing fresh silt and moisture to the small irregular fields of the Quechan, in which were grown several varieties of maize (corn), as well as pumpkins, melons, beans, and grasses. In addition to their plentiful harvests, they gathered seeds and fruits, hunted small game, and fished.

Most contemporary Quechan live on the Fort Yuma–Quechan Reservation near Yuma, Ariz., west of the Colorado River. It borders Mexico and California. Some of the reservation land is still farmed. The Fort Yuma–Quechan Museum, established in what was once the Fort Yuma officer's mess, presents a history of the tribe and its relations with early Spanish missionaries and explorers and the American military. The Quechan own and operate casinos and a number of other small enterprises mostly related to tourism. In the early 21st century, descendants of the Quechan numbered some 2,500.

Pima and Tohono O'odham (Uto-Aztecan Speakers)

The Uto-Aztecan family of languages is spoken in Mexico and northern Guatemala, as well as the southwestern United States. The Uto-Aztecan languages are generally recognized by modern linguists as falling into eight branches: Numic, Takic, Hopi, and Tubatulabal, which some scholars consider to make up Northern Uto-Aztecan; and Pimic, Taracahitic, Cora-Huichol, and Aztecan.

PIMA

The Pima traditionally lived along the Gila and Salt rivers in Arizona, in what was the core area of the prehistoric Hohokam culture. The Pima, who call themselves the "River People," are usually considered to be the descendants of the Hohokam. Like their presumed ancestors, the Pima were traditionally sedentary farmers who lived in one-room houses and utilized the rivers for irrigation. Some hunting and gathering were done to supplement the diet, and in drought years, which occurred on the average of one year in five, crop failure made hunting and gathering the sole mode of subsistence. During these dry years jackrabbits and mesquite beans became the group's dietary staples.

The intensive farming of the Pima made possible larger villages than were feasible for their neighbours and relatives, the Tohono O'odham. With larger communities came a stronger and more complex political organization. In the early Spanish colonial period the Pima possessed a strong tribal organization, with a tribal chief elected by the chiefs of the various villages. The tribal and local chiefs attained their status through their personal qualities rather than through birth. The village chief, aided by a council of all adult males, had the responsibilities of directing the communal irrigation projects and of protecting the village against alien tribes, notably the Apache. Planting and harvesting crops were handled as a cooperative venture.

From the time of their earliest recorded contacts with European and American colonizers, the Pima have been regarded as a friendly people. During the California Gold

Rush (1849–50), the Pima often gave or sold food to emigrant settlers and gold seekers and provided them with an escort through Apache territory. During the Apache wars (1861–86), some Pima served as scouts for the U.S. Army.

In the early 21st century Pima descendants numbered some 11,000.

Tohono O'odham (Papago)

The Tohono O'odham traditionally inhabited the desert regions of present-day Arizona and northern Sonora, Mex. Culturally they are similar to the Pima living to the north. There are, however, certain dissimilarities. The drier territory of the Tohono O'odham made farming difficult and increased the tribe's reliance on wild foods. They moved seasonally because of the arid climate, spending the summer in "field villages" and the winter in "well villages."

Traditionally, unlike the Pima, the Tohono O'odham did not store water to irrigate their fields, instead practicing a form of flash-flood farming. After the first rains, they planted seeds in the alluvial fans at the mouths of washes that marked the maximum reach of the water after flash floods. Because the floods could be heavy, it was necessary for the seeds to be planted deeply, usually 4 to 6 inches (10–15 cm) into the soil. Reservoirs, ditches, and dikes were constructed to slow and impound runoff waters along the flood channels. Women were responsible for gathering wild foods.

The shifting residential pattern and wide dispersal of the Tohono O'odham fields kept villages small and lessened the desirability of a unified tribal political organization. The largest organizational unit appears to have been a group of related villages. The Tohono O'odham had much less contact with settlers than the Pima and in general retained more of their traditional culture.

Early 21st-century population estimates indicated more than 20,000 individuals of Tohono O'odham descent.

PUEBLO INDIANS

Pueblo Indians are so called because they live in compact permanent settlements known as pueblos. Most live in northeastern Arizona and northwestern New Mexico. Pueblo peoples are thought to be the descendants of the prehistoric Ancestral Pueblo (Anasazi) culture. Just as there was considerable regional diversity among the Ancestral Pueblo, there is similar diversity, both cultural and linguistic, among the Pueblo. Contemporary Puebloans are customarily described as belonging to either the eastern or the western division.

The eastern Pueblo villages are in New Mexico along the Rio Grande and comprise groups who speak Tanoan

Taos Pueblo, N.M., with domed oven in the foreground. Ray Manley/ Shostal Associates

and Keresan languages. Tanoan languages such as Tewa are distantly related to Uto-Aztecan, but Keresan has no known affinities. The western Pueblos include the Hopi villages of northern Arizona and the Zuni, Acoma, and Laguna villages, all in western New Mexico. Of the western Pueblos, Acoma and Laguna speak Keresan. The Zuni speak Zuni, a language of Penutian affiliation. And the Hopi Pueblos, with one exception, speak Hopi, a Uto-Aztecan language. The exception is the village of Hano, which is composed of Tewa refugees from the Rio Grande.

Traditional social and religious practices are fairly well understood for the western Pueblo peoples because distance and the rugged landscape of the Colorado Plateau afforded them some protection from the depredations of Spanish, and later American, colonizers. Less is known of the pre-conquest practices of the eastern Pueblos. Their location on the banks of the Rio Grande made them easily accessible to colonizers, whose approaches to assimilation were often brutal. Many Pueblos, both eastern and western, took their traditional practices underground during the colonial period in order to avoid persecution. To a great extent they continue to protect their traditional cultures with silence. Their secret societies, each of which

Pueblo Indian pottery: (left) *Acoma water jar, c. 1890,* (centre) *Santa Clara vase, c. 1880, and* (right) *San Ildefonso water jar, c. 1906.* Courtesy of the Denver Art Museum, Denver, Colorado

had a specific theme such as religion, war, policing, hunting, or healing, have proven quite difficult to investigate. Undoubtedly, however, they were and are important venues for social interaction and cultural transmission.

The Pueblo peoples resided in multifamily buildings. The women of a household cared for young children; cultivated spring-irrigated gardens; produced fine baskets and pottery; had charge of the preservation, storage, and cooking of food; and cared for certain clan fetishes (sacred objects carved of stone). The men of a household wove cloth, herded sheep, and raised field and dune crops of maize (corn), squash, beans, and cotton. A wide trade network brought materials such as turquoise, shell, copper, and macaw feathers to the Pueblo tribes. Many of these exotic materials appear to have come from Mexico.

The family was a key social grouping. Extended family households of three generations were typical. The western Pueblos and the eastern Keresan-speaking groups reckoned kinship through the female line (matrilineally), while the remaining eastern Pueblos reckoned kinship patrilineally or bilaterally, through both parents. Residence usually coincided with kinship. Among the matrilineal Zuni, for instance, a husband joined his wife's natal residence (matrilocality). A Zuni household would typically include a senior woman, her husband, and their unmarried children, plus the couple's married daughters, sons-in-law, and their children.

Related families formed a lineage, a kin group that could trace its ancestry directly to a known figure in the historical or legendary past. Lineages were often conceived of as timeless, extending backward into the remote past and forward through generations yet unborn. Among the western Pueblo and the eastern Keresan-speakers, several related lineages were combined to form a clan. Many villages had dozens of clans, which were often named for animals, plants, or other natural phenomena.

Instead of using clans, some Pueblos grouped lineages directly into two units called moieties. This was particularly prevalent among the eastern Pueblos, many of whom organized themselves into paired groups such as the Squash People and Turquoise People or the Summer People and Winter People. These groups alternate responsibility for pueblo activities, and their secret societies deal primarily with curing rituals. In contrast, the western Pueblos are organized into several matrilineal lineages and clans. Secret societies, each controlled by a particular clan, perform a calendrical cycle of rituals to ensure rain and tribal welfare.

Clans and moieties acted as corporate groups. They were responsible for sponsoring certain rituals and for organizing many aspects of community life. Among the matrilineal Hopi, for instance, each clan owned specific fields and ritual paraphernalia and the oldest active woman functioned as the clan's administrative leader. Her brother assumed the responsibilities of ceremonial leader, supervising annual reenactments of events that were part of clan history or tradition. At San Juan pueblo in the east, the kinship system was bilateral, and the fluidity inherent in a bilateral system was reflected in the moiety system as well: one was born into membership in one's father's moiety, but upon marriage a young woman became a member of her husband's division. At San Juan the leaders of the Summer and the Winter moieties were each responsible for village administration during their respective season (spring and summer were grouped together, as were autumn and winter). Many activities were limited to just one of the seasons. Trading and hunting, for instance, could only take place under the authority of the Winter moiety, while the gathering of wild plants was limited to the period of the Summer People's administration.

Clan and moiety systems were important tools for managing the delegation of ritual and mundane tasks, but were also important in achieving harmony in other ways. Membership in these groups was symbolically extended to specific animals, plants, and other classes of natural and supernatural phenomena, metaphysically linking all aspects of the social, natural, and spiritual worlds together for a given tribe. In a concrete political sense as well, the common (though not universal) custom of clan or moiety exogamy, or out-marriage, smoothed social relations by ensuring that households included members of different corporate groups.

Each of the 70 or more Pueblo villages extant before Spanish colonization was politically autonomous, governed by a council composed of the heads of religious societies. These societies were centred in the kivas, subterranean ceremonial chambers that also functioned as private clubs

Group of Pueblo Indians playing a game, 1890. Library of Congress, Washington, D.C.

and lounging rooms for men. Traditionally, Pueblo peoples were farmers, with the types of farming and associated traditions of property ownership varying among the groups. Along the Rio Grande and its tributaries maize (corn) and cotton were cultivated in irrigated fields in river bottoms. Among the western Pueblos, especially the Hopi, farming was less reliable because there were few permanent water sources. Traditionally, women did most of the farming, but as hunting has diminished in importance, men have also become responsible for agricultural work. Many of the Rio Grande Pueblos had special hunting societies that hunted deer and antelope in the mountains, and easterly Pueblos such as the Taos and Picurís sometimes sent hunters to the Plains for bison. Among all Pueblos communal rabbit hunts were held, and women gathered wild plants to eat.

In 1539 a Franciscan friar, Marcos de Niza, claimed the Pueblo region for Spain. Explorer Francisco Vázquez de Coronado followed in 1540, quickly and brutally pacifying all indigenous resistance. In 1680 a Tewa man, Popé, led the Pueblo Rebellion against the Spanish. The colonizers retreated from the region for several years but completed a reconquest in 1691. Subsequently, most villages adapted to colonial rule through syncretism, adopting and incorporating those aspects of the dominant culture necessary for survival under its regime, while maintaining the basic fabric of traditional culture. Historical examples of Pueblo syncretism include the addition of sheep and shepherding to the agricultural economy and the adoption of some Christian religious practices.

Contemporary Pueblo peoples continue to use syncretic strategies. They have adopted a variety of modern convenience products, yet extensively retain their traditional kinship systems, religions, and crafts. Social life centres on the village, which is also the primary political unit. Kinship plays a fundamental role in social and religious life in 21st-century Pueblo communities. It may delimit an individual's potential marriage partners and often determines eligibility for membership in religious societies and a wide variety of social and economic obligations.

Early 21st-century population estimates indicated approximately 75,000 individuals of Pueblo descent.

HOPI (UTO-AZTECAN)

Also called Moki (or Moqui), the Hopi constitute the westernmost group of Pueblo Indians, situated in what is now northeastern Arizona, on the edge of the Painted Desert.

The precise origin of the Hopi is unknown, although (as mentioned above) they are believed to have descended from the Ancestral Pueblo (Anasazi), whom the Hopi call Hisatsinom ("Ancient People"). Archaeology has revealed that some abandoned pueblos, such as Sikyatki and Awatovi, were once occupied by Hopi people. Hopi origin traditions tell that their ancestors climbed upward through underground chambers called kivas and lived in many places before reaching their present settlements in this, the Fourth World.

Traditional Hopi culture emphasized monogamy and matrilineal descent. Hopi people also practiced matrilocal residence, in which a new husband becomes part of his mother-in-law's household. A given pueblo, or town, might include two dozen or more matrilineal clans. These were grouped into several larger social units, or phratries.

The traditional Hopi economy centred on farming and, after Spanish colonization, on herding sheep. The chief crop was maize (corn), and the Hopi also grew beans, squash, melons, and a variety of other vegetables and fruits. Men farmed and herded, in addition to building houses, performing most of the ceremonies, making moccasins, and weaving garments and blankets. Women made baskets and pottery, gardened, raised children, cared for the elderly, and were responsible for the strenuous tasks of providing their families with hand-drawn water and hand-ground cornmeal.

Girls and boys began their ceremonial careers soon after reaching six years of age by being inducted into the kachina religious tradition. Hopi kachinas represented a wide variety of gods, spirits, departed ancestors, and clouds. During certain ceremonies they were impersonated by men in elaborate regalia. Women generally took the role of observers during the public aspects of ceremonies, except in events involving one or more of the three women's societies. Men also had the option of joining a number of societies, including those that conducted a strenuous tribal initiation and staged an annual winter solstice celebration, or soyal. So important was the soyal that its leadership was always entrusted to a high official, usually the town's chief.

The most widely publicized of Hopi rituals was the Snake Dance, held annually in late August, during which the performers danced with live snakes in their mouths. Although

Hopi Snake Dance, *watercolour by Awa Tsireh,* c. *1920.* Courtesy of the Denver Art Museum, Denver, Colorado

part of the Snake Dance was performed in public, visitors saw only a brief, though exciting, portion of a lengthy ceremony, most of which was conducted privately in kivas.

Some aspects of Hopi life have been considerably affected as a result of Spanish, and later American, colonization. Foremost among these are land disputes between the Hopi and the neighbouring Navajo. However, many aspects of traditional Hopi life persisted into the early 21st century. At that time, terraced pueblo structures of stone and adobe continued to dominate the architecture of a number of independent Hopi towns. Kachina religion remained vibrant, and a strong craft tradition persists in Hopi communities.

Early 21st-century population estimates indicated more than 15,000 individuals of Hopi descent.

ZUNI (PENUTIAN)

Living in what is now west-central New Mexico, on the Arizona border, the Zuni (sometimes spelled Zuñi) also are believed to be descendants of the prehistoric Ancestral Pueblo (Anasazi). Like those of the Hopi, Zuni traditions depict a past in which their ancestors emerged from underground and eventually settled at the tribe's present location.

When Pueblo tribes first encountered Spanish colonizers in the 16th century, the Zuni were living in Hawikuh and five or six other towns. Collectively these towns came to be called the Seven Cities of Cibola, host to a rumoured empire of gold that was sought in vain by Francisco Vázquez de Coronado and other conquistadors. The Zuni also participated in the Pueblo Rebellion and like the other Pueblo Indians retained their independence until 1691, when the Spanish reconquered the area.

Zuni society is organized through kinship and includes 13 matrilineal clans. Like other Pueblo peoples, the Zuni are deeply religious and have a complex ceremonial organization and a religious life centred on kachinas.

Most Zunis farm, raising maize (corn), squash, and beans. Since the early 19th century the Zuni have been known for making silver and turquoise jewelry, baskets, beadwork, animal fetishes, and pottery. Many Zuni have chosen to adopt only some parts of modern American life and to maintain much of their traditional culture.

In the early 21st century the population of Zuni Pueblo was some 10,000 individuals.

APACHEANS (ATHABASKAN SPEAKERS)

While the peoples mentioned thus far all have very ancient roots in the Southwest, the Navajo and Apache are relative newcomers. Linguistic, archaeological, and historical evidence indicate that the ancestors of these groups were members of hunting-and-gathering cultures that migrated to the region from present-day Canada, arriving by approximately 1500 CE, although no earlier than 1100 CE. The Navajo occupied a portion of the Colorado Plateau adjacent to Hopi lands. The Apache claimed the basin and range country east and south of the Plateau and surrounding the Rio Grande pueblos. Together, the Navajo and Apache are referred to as Apacheans.

Their origins in what is now Canada are indicated by the languages they speak, called Athabaskan and also spelled Athabaskan, Athabascan, Athapaskan, or Athapascan. The Proto-Athabaskan *Urheimat*, or original homeland, is thought to have been a northern area with a watershed that drained into the Pacific Ocean, such as eastern Alaska or western Yukon. The languages in this family are spoken in three discontinuous geographic regions: the Pacific Coast, northwestern Canada and the

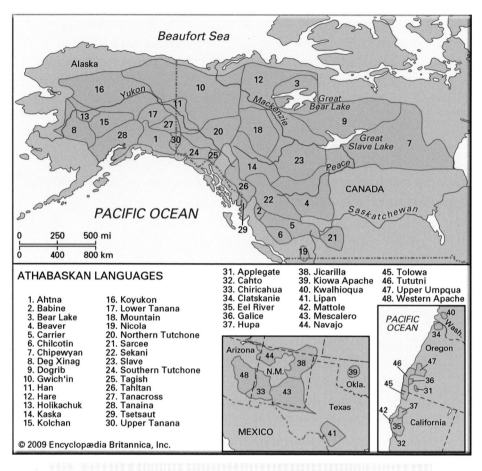

Distribution of Athabaskan languages.

Alaskan interior, and the southwestern United States, home to the Apachean subgroup, which includes Navajo and the languages spoken by the Apache peoples.

By the early 17th century the Navajo and the Jicarilla, Lipan, and Western Apache had begun to engage in a relatively settled way of life, farming indigenous crops. After the advent of Spanish colonization, they incorporated new products such as sheep and cattle into their economies. The Chiricahua and Mescalero Apache continued to rely on hunting and gathering as the mainstay of their economies. All the groups raided the Pueblo tribes and later the Spanish and American colonizers. Raids were often (although not always) undertaken in stealth, as the goal was generally to seize livestock and food stores rather than to engage in battle.

In general, Apachean women were responsible for raising their children. They also gathered and processed edible seeds and other wild plants, such as mescal, a cactus that provided food, juice, and fibres; collected water and firewood; produced pottery, baskets, and buckskin clothing; and built the home. The Navajo were an exception to the last rule, as they viewed home construction as men's work. Apachean men hunted, fought, and raided. Among the more sedentary groups, women tended gardens, men tended fields, and both engaged in shepherding and weaving.

As their territories were generally unfavourable to the support of concentrated populations, the Apacheans tended to reside in dispersed groups. Although the Navajo and Western Apache had some matrilineal clans, kinship was generally reckoned bilaterally and clans played little role among most Apachean groups. The basic socioeconomic unit was the matrilocal extended family, a group of one or more related women, their husbands and unmarried sons, and their daughters, sons-in-law, and grandchildren. Within this group each nuclear family—or each wife and her children, if two or more women shared a husband—occupied a separate dwelling. Among the Navajo the preferred house form was the hogan, a circular lodge made of logs or stone and covered with a roof of earth. Some hogans also had earth-berm walls. Among the Apache, the wickiup and tepee were used. The ramada, a freestanding rectangular arbour, was used by both groups for shade.

Among the Apache, a kin-based group of perhaps 20–30 individuals who lived and worked together constituted a band, the most important social group in daily life. Among the Navajo, similarly sized "outfits," or neighbouring extended families, cooperated in resolving issues such as range management and water use. Bands and outfits were organized under the direction of a leader chosen for his wisdom and previous success. They functioned on the basis of consensus, and individuals could, and often did, move to another group if they were uncomfortable with their current situation. A tribe comprised a group of bands that shared bonds of tradition, language, and culture. They were usually not formal political entities. The small bands that functioned as basic social units should not be confused with larger groups, such as the Mescalero, that are sometimes referred to as bands but are in fact tribes.

APACHE

The Apache, under such leaders as Cochise, Mangas Coloradas, Geronimo, and Victorio, figured largely in the history of the Southwest during the latter half of the 19th century. Their name is probably derived from a Spanish transliteration of *ápachu*, the term for "enemy" in Zuñi.

Before Spanish colonization, Apache domain extended over what are now (in the United States) east-central and southeastern Arizona, southeastern Colorado, southwestern and eastern New Mexico, and western Texas and (in Mexico) northern Chihuahua and Sonora states.

Although the Apache eventually chose to adopt a nomadic way of life that relied heavily on horse transport, semisedentary Plains Apache farmers were living along the Dismal River in what is now Kansas as recently as 1700. When the horse and gun trades converged in the central Plains about 1750, guerrilla-style raiding by previously nomadic groups such as the Comanche greatly increased. The remaining Plains Apache were severely pressured and retreated to the south and west.

Culturally, the Apache are divided into Eastern Apache, which include the Mescalero, Jicarilla, Chiricahua, Lipan, and Kiowa Apache, and Western Apache, which include the Cibecue, Mimbreño, Coyotero, and Northern and Southern Tonto or Mogollon Apache. With the exception of the Kiowa Apache, who joined the Kiowa tribal circle (adopting Kiowa customs and allegiance), the Apache traditionally functioned without a centralized tribal organization. Instead, the band, an autonomous small group within a given locality, was the primary political unit as well as the primary raiding unit. The strongest headman of a band was recognized as an informal chief, and several bands might be united under one leader. Chieftainship was thus an earned privilege rather than a hereditary one.

Once the Apache had moved to the Southwest, they developed a flexible subsistence economy that included hunting and gathering wild foods, farming, and obtaining food and other items from Pueblo villages via trade, livestock hunts, and raiding. The proportion of each activity varied greatly from tribe to tribe. The Jicarilla farmed fairly extensively, growing maize (corn) and other vegetables, and hunted bison extensively. The Lipan of Texas, who were probably originally a band of Jicarilla, had largely given up farming for a more mobile lifestyle. The Mescalero were influenced by the Plains tribes' corn- and bison-based economies, but their chief food staple was the mescal plant (hence the name Mescalero). The Chiricahua were perhaps the most nomadic and aggressive of the Apache west of the Rio Grande, raiding into northern Mexico, Arizona, and New Mexico from their strongholds in the Dragoon Mountains. The Western Apache appear to have been more settled than their Eastern relatives. Although their economy emphasized farming, they did raid fully sedentary tribes frequently. One of the Western Apache tribes, the Navajo, traded extensively with the

Pueblo tribes and was heavily influenced by these firmly agriculturist cultures.

Although they were among the fiercest groups on the colonial frontiers of Mexico and the United States, and perhaps because of their confidence in their own military prowess, the Apache initially attempted to be friends of the Spanish, Mexicans, and Americans. As early as the 17th century, however, Apache bands were raiding Spanish missions. The Spanish failure to protect missionized Pueblo villages from Apache raids during a five-year drought in the late 17th century may have helped to instigate the Pueblo Rebellion of 1680. During the Spanish retaliation immediately following the revolt, many Pueblo individuals took shelter with the Navajo.

In 1858 a meeting at Apache Pass in the Dragoon Mountains between the Americans and the Chiricahua Apache resulted in a peace that lasted until 1861, when Cochise went on the warpath. This marked the beginning of 25 years of confrontation between U.S. military forces and the native peoples of the Southwest. The causes of the conflict included the Apache disinclination toward reservation life and incursions onto Apache lands that were related to the development of gold, silver, and coal mining operations in the region. The latter often took place with the consent of corrupt Office of Indian Affairs staff.

Despite their adept use of swift horses and their knowledge of the terrain, the Apache were eventually outmatched by the superior arms of American troops. The Navajo surrendered in 1865 and agreed to settle on a reservation in New Mexico. Other Apache groups ostensibly followed suit in 1871–73, but large numbers of warriors refused to yield their nomadic ways and accept permanent confinement. Thus, intermittent raids continued to be led by such Apache leaders as Geronimo and Victorio, evoking federal action once more.

COCHISE

(d. June 8, 1874, Chiricahua Apache Reservation, Arizona Territory, U.S.)

The Chiricahua Apache chief Cochise led the Indians' resistance to Euro-American incursions into the U.S. Southwest in the 1860s. The southeasternmost county of Arizona bears his name.

Nothing is known of Cochise's birth or early life. His people remained at peace with white settlers through the 1850s, even working as woodcutters at the Apache Pass stagecoach station. Trouble began in 1861, when a raiding party drove off cattle belonging to a white rancher and abducted the child of a ranch hand. An inexperienced U.S. Army officer ordered Cochise and five other chiefs to appear for questioning. Steadfastly denying their guilt, the Indians were seized and arrested. One was killed on the spot, but Cochise escaped by cutting through the side of a tent, despite three bullets in his body. Immediately he laid plans to avenge the death of his friends, who had been hanged by federal authorities. The warfare of his Apache bands was so fierce that troops, settlers, and traders alike were all forced to withdraw. Upon the recall of army forces to fight in the U.S. Civil War (1861–65), Arizona was practically abandoned to the Apaches.

In 1862, however, an army of 3,000 California volunteers under Gen. James Carleton marched to Apache Pass to reestablish communications between the Pacific coast and the East, putting the Indians to flight with their howitzers.

Upon the death of his co-fighter and father-in-law Mangas Coloradas (chief of the Mimbreño Apaches), Cochise became principal chief of the Apaches. From that time on a war of extermination was waged against the Indians. Cochise and 200 followers eluded capture for more than 10 years by hiding out in the Dragoon Mountains of Arizona, from which they continued their raids, always melting back into their mountain strongholds.

In June 1871 command of the Department of Arizona was assumed by Gen. George Crook, who succeeded in winning the allegiance of a number of Apaches as scouts and bringing many others onto reservations. Cochise surrendered in September,

but, resisting the transfer of his people to the Tularosa
Reservation in New Mexico, he escaped in the spring of 1872.
He gave himself up when the Chiricahua Reservation was estab-
lished that summer.

The last of the Apache wars ended in 1886 with the surrender of Geronimo and his few remaining followers. The
Chiricahua tribe was evacuated from the West and held
as prisoners of war successively in Florida, in Alabama,
and at Ft. Sill, Okla., for a total of 27 years. In 1913 the
members of the tribe were given the choice of taking
allotments of land in Oklahoma or living in New Mexico
on the Mescalero Reservation. Approximately one-third
chose the former and two-thirds the latter.

Apache descendants totaled some 100,000 individuals in the early 21st century.

NAVAJO

The Navajo (also spelled Navaho) are the second most
populous of Native American people in the United States,
with some 300,000 individuals in the early 21st century,
most of them living in New Mexico, Arizona, and Utah.

Although the exact timing of the Navajo relocation to
this region is unknown, it is thought to have been between
1100 and 1500 CE. These early Navajo were mobile hunters
and gatherers, but they soon adopted many of the practices of the sedentary, farming Pueblo Indians near whom
they settled.

Navajo interactions with Pueblo tribes were recorded
at least as early as the 17th century, when refugees from
some of the Rio Grande pueblos came to the Navajo after
the Spanish suppression of the Pueblo Revolt. During the
18th century, some Hopi tribal members left their mesas

because of drought and famine and joined with the Navajo, particularly in Canyon de Chelly in northeast Arizona. Pueblo artistic influences drew Navajo people to adopt painted pottery and weaving. Navajo rugs are particularly esteemed. Elements of Navajo ceremonialism such as dry-sand painting are also products of these contacts. Another important Navajo artistic tradition, the creation of silver jewelry, dates from the middle of the 19th century and was probably first learned from Mexican smiths.

Navajo religion is widely practiced and notable for its intricacy. Some of its many traditions relate the emergence of the first people from various worlds beneath the surface of the earth. Other stories explain the origins and purposes of numerous rites and ceremonies. Some of these are simple rituals carried out by individuals or families for luck in travel and trade or for the protection of crops and herds. More-complex rites involve a specialist who is paid according to the complexity and length of the ceremonial. Traditionally, most rites were primarily for curing physical and mental illness. In other ceremonies there were simply prayers or songs, and dry paintings might be made of pollen and flower petals. In some cases there were public dances and exhibitions at which hundreds or thousands of Navajo gathered. Many of these rites are still performed.

Although the Navajo never raided as extensively as the Apache, their activities caused the U.S. government in 1863 to order Col. Kit Carson to subdue them. The ensuing campaign resulted in the destruction of large amounts of crops and herds and the incarceration of about 8,000 Navajo, along with 400 Mescalero Apache, at Bosque Redondo, 180 miles (290 km) south of Santa Fe, N.M. This four-year (1864–68) captivity left a legacy of bitterness and distrust that has still not entirely disappeared.

The Navajo resemble other Apachean peoples in their general preference for limiting centralized tribal or political organization, although they have adopted pan-tribal governmental and legal systems in order to maintain tribal sovereignty. Traditional Navajo society was organized through matrilineal kinship. Small, independent bands of related kin generally made decisions on a consensus basis. Similar groups still exist but tend to be based on locality of residence as well as kinship. Many of these local groups have elected leaders. A local group is not a village or town but rather a collection of dwellings or hamlets distributed over a wide area.

In the early 21st century many Navajo continued to live a predominantly traditional lifestyle, speaking the Navajo language, practicing the religion, and organizing through traditional forms of social structure. Navajo men and women also continued the tradition of volunteering for the armed services at a high rate, perhaps as an expression of a cultural ethic that emphasizes both personal competence and community. In maintaining these disparate traditions, the Navajo have been cultural innovators. For example, the Navajo code talkers of World War II—Marines who used their native language to foil enemy monitoring of vital communications—played a definitive role in winning the war (and saved countless lives) by maintaining crucial radio contact on the battlefield.

Many Navajo continue to live in the area they settled centuries ago. In the early 21st century their reservation and government-allotted lands in New Mexico, Arizona, and Utah totaled more than 24,000 square miles (64,000 square km). The region is mainly arid, however, and generally will not support enough agriculture and livestock to provide a livelihood for all of its residents. Thousands earn their living away from the Navajo country, and appreciable numbers have settled on irrigated lands along the lower Colorado River and in such places as Los Angeles, Calif., and Kansas City, Mo.

CONCLUSION

As has been noted, a map of the peoples of California, the Great Basin, and the Southwest reveals a noteworthy patchwork. A study of the languages spoken and variety of ways of life provides a fascinating history of migration and settlement, of influence and persistence. Perhaps of the three groups of Native Americans presented here, the California Indians differ most from the popular image of Indians that prevailed into the mid-20th century. The northern groups, like many Northwest Coast tribes, held first-fruits ceremonies based on salmon, which they considered supernatural beings who voluntarily assumed fish form to sacrifice themselves annually for the benefit of humankind. On being taken, the spirits of the fish returned to their home beneath the sea, where they were reincarnated if their bones were returned to the water. If offended, however, the salmon-beings would refuse to return to the river. Hence, there were numerous specific prohibitions on acts believed to offend them and observances designed to propitiate them.

By the same token, the Great Basin and Southwest Indians conform most to the stereotype often held. Many groups used bows, arrows, and horses, and fought many bloody battles against encroachment and confinement to reservations. Yet their strategies for daily life were infinitely variable, down to the decorations on the clothes they wore and the nature of the shelters they built.

Yet one quality unites the many groups of these culture areas. Each exhibits a remarkable steadfastness in the face of centuries of broken treaties, bad faith negotiations, and various other harsh realities they have faced.

agglutination The use of prefixes, suffixes, and other meaningful word elements to form a single long, complex word.

dentalium Any of a genus of tapered marine mollusk shells that resemble an animal's tooth or tusk.

fetish An object (as a small stone carving of an animal) believed to have magical power to protect or aid its owner.

hogan A Navajo Indian dwelling usually made of logs and mud with a door traditionally facing east.

kachina Divine, ancestral spirit beings who interact with humans; often represented by doll figures.

kiva A subterranean ceremonial chamber that also functioned as a private gathering space for Pueblo men.

levirate A custom in which a man wed his dead brother's widow and took on the responsibility of providing for her and her children.

matrilineal Based on the mother's heritage and familial lines.

moiety A subdivision in a society that has a complementary counterpart.

patrilineal Based on the father's heritage and familial lines.

petroglyph Drawings etched into rock by ancient peoples as a form of communication or record.

peyote A hallucinogenic drug obtained from the mescal cactus.

phratry A tribal subsection based on the division of clans.

potlatch A ceremony marking a special occasion where the social status of members of certain Native American tribes was established or announced by the giving of gifts.

ramada A roofed shelter with usually open sides.

reification The act or process of regarding (something abstract) as a material or concrete thing.

shaman A priest or priestess who has shown an exceptionally strong affinity with the spirit world. Shamans are also considered healers and are thought to be adept at divination.

sororate The marriage of one man to two or more sisters, usually successively and after the first wife has been found to be barren or after her death.

sweat lodge A hut, lodge, or cavern heated by steam from water poured on hot stones; used ritualistically by Native American tribes.

syncretic The fusion of different systems of belief, as in religion or philosophy.

toloache A narcotic annual herb (especially *Datura meteloides*) used ceremonially by some indigenous peoples of California.

wattle and daub A framework of woven rods and twigs covered and plastered with clay and used in building construction.

wickiup A dome-shaped form of lodging favoured by certain Native American peoples, constructed by draping bent saplings with rushes or bark.

BIBLIOGRAPHY

Classic syntheses of the traditional cultures of the California Indians include A.L. Kroeber, *Handbook of the Indians of California* (1925, reprinted 1975); Robert F. Heizer and M.A. Whipple (compilers and eds.), *The California Indians: A Source Book*, 2nd ed., rev. and enlarged (1971); Lowell John Bean and Thomas C. Blackburn (eds.), *Native Californians: A Theoretical Retrospective* (1976); William C. Sturtevant (ed.), *Handbook of North American Indians*, vol. 8, *California*, ed. by Robert F. Heizer (1978); Robert F. Heizer and Albert B. Elsasser, *The Natural World of the California Indians* (1980); and Jack D. Forbes, *Native Americans of California and Nevada*, rev. ed. (1982).

Descriptions of particular cultures include Raymond C. White, *Luiseño Social Organization* (1963, reissued 1971); Lowell John Bean, *Mukat's People: The Cahuilla Indians of Southern California* (1972); and Virginia P. Miller, *Ukomnóm: The Yuki Indians of Northern California* (1979). Very readable books for the nonspecialist are Theodora Kroeber, *Ishi in Two Worlds* (1961, reissued 1976); and Theodora Kroeber and Robert F. Heizer, *Almost Ancestors: The First Californians* (1968).

Histories of Native California that illuminate issues of colonial conquest and indigenous identity include Robert F. Heizer and Alan F. Almquist, *The Other Californians: Prejudice and Discrimination Under Spain, Mexico, and the United States to 1920* (1971); George Harwood Phillips, *Chiefs and Challengers: Indian Resistance and Cooperation in Southern California* (1975); Sherburne F. Cook, *The Population of the California Indians, 1769–1970* (1976); Albert L. Hurtado,

Indian Survival on the California Frontier (1988); Clifford E. Trafzer and Joel R. Hyer (eds.), *Exterminate Them: Written Accounts of the Murder, Rape, and Slavery of Native Americans During the California Gold Rush, 1848–1868* (1999); Joel R. Hyer, *We Are Not Savages: Native Americans in Southern California and the Pala Reservation, 1840–1920* (2001); George Harwood Phillips, *Bringing Them Under Subjection: California's Tejón Indian Reservation and Beyond, 1852–1864* (2004); James A. Sandos, *Converting California: Indians and Franciscans in the Missions* (2004); and Kent G. Lightfoot, *Indians, Missionaries, and Merchants: The Legacy of Colonial Encounters on the California Frontiers* (2005).

Native California life in the 20th and 21st centuries is discussed in Thomas Buckley, *Standing Ground: Yurok Indian Spirituality, 1850–1990* (2002); and Susan Lobo et al. (eds.), *Urban Voices: The Bay Area American Indian Community* (2002).

There is no general monograph on all Great Basin Indians, but William C. Sturtevant (ed.), *Handbook of the North American Indians*, vol. 11, *Great Basin*, ed. by Warren L. d'Azevedo (1986), provides summary articles on various groups and aspects of Great Basin anthropology; it also updates the approximately 6,500 references listed in Catherine S. Fowler (compiler), *Great Basin Anthropology: A Bibliography* (1970).

There are many descriptions of particular Great Basin cultures. The earliest systematic study of Great Basin Indians was by John Wesley Powell; his work is detailed in Don D. Fowler and Catherine S. Fowler (eds.), *Anthropology of the Numa: John Wesley Powell's Manuscripts on the Numic Peoples of Western North America, 1868–1880* (1971). Ethnographic studies from the 20th century include Julian H. Steward, *Basin-Plateau Aboriginal Sociopolitical Groups* (1938, reprinted 1970 and later); Robert F. Murphy and Yolanda Murphy, *Shoshone-Bannock Subsistence and*

Society (1960, reprinted 1976); Virginia Cole Trenholm and Maurine Carley, *The Shoshonis: Sentinels of the Rockies* (1964, reissued 1981); James F. Downs, *The Two Worlds of the Washo, an Indian Tribe of California and Nevada* (1966); Isabel T. Kelly, *Ethnography of the Surprise Valley Paiute* (1932), and *Southern Paiute Ethnography* (1964, reprinted 1976); and Catherine S. Fowler, *In the Shadow of Fox Peak: Ethnography of the Cattail-Eater Northern Paiute People of Stillwater Marsh* (1992).

Religious beliefs are treated by Willard Z. Park, *Shamanism in Western North America: A Study in Cultural Relationships* (1938, reprinted 1975); Beatrice Blyth Whiting, *Paiute Sorcery* (1950, reprinted 1971); Michael Hittman (compiler), *Wovoka and the Ghost Dance* (1990); and Jason Baird Jackson, *Yuchi Ceremonial Life: Performance, Meaning, and Tradition in a Contemporary American Indian Community* (2003).

The histories of indigenous Great Basin peoples are explored in Steven J. Crum, *The Road on Which We Came: A History of the Western Shoshone* (1994); Martha C. Knack, *Boundaries Between: The Southern Paiutes, 1775–1995* (2001); Timothy Braatz, *Surviving Conquest: A History of the Yavapai Peoples* (2003); and Ned Blackhawk, *Violence Over the Land: Indians and Empires in the Early American West* (2006).

Regional syntheses of the traditional cultures of the Southwest include William C. Sturtevant (ed.), *Handbook of North American Indians*, vol. 9 and 10, *Southwest*, ed. by Alfonso Ortiz (1979–83); Linda S. Cordell, *Prehistory of the Southwest* (1984); and Trudy Griffin-Pierce, *Native Peoples of the Southwest* (2000), and *The Columbia Guide to American Indians of the Southwest* (2007).

Syntheses of particular aspects of Southwest Indian culture and history include 19th-century U.S. Army surgeon Washington Matthews, *Navaho Myths Prayers and*

Songs, ed. by P.E. Goddard (1907, reprinted 1964); Edward H. Spicer, *Cycles of Conquest: The Impact of Spain, Mexico, and the United States on the Indians of the Southwest, 1533–1960* (1962); John Collier and Ira Muskowitz, *Patterns and Ceremonials of the Indians of the Southwest* (1949, reissued as *American Indian Ceremonial Dances*, 1972); Ruth M. Underhill, *Ceremonial Patterns in the Greater Southwest* (1948, reissued 1966); Steven A. LeBlanc, *Prehistoric Warfare in the American Southwest* (1999); James F. Brooks, *Captives & Cousins: Slavery, Kinship, and Community in the Southwest Borderlands* (2002); and R. Warren Metcalf, *Termination's Legacy: The Discarded Indians of Utah* (2002).

Classic studies of tribes in the western and southern areas within the region include C. Daryll Forde, *Ethnography of the Yuma Indians* (1931, reissued 1965); Leslie Spier, *Yuman Tribes of the Gila River* (1933, reprinted 1978); Ruth M. Underhill, *Singing for Power: The Song Magic of the Papago Indians of Southern Arizona* (1938, reissued 1993); Alice Joseph, Rosamond B. Spicer, and Jane Chesky, *The Desert People* (1949, reprinted 1974), also on the Tohono O'odham (Pima-Papago); and William H. Kelly, *The Papago Indians of Arizona* (1963, reissued 1974).

Studies of Pueblo tribes include Elsie Clews Parsons, *Pueblo Indian Religion*, 2 vol. (1939, reprinted 1974); Fred Eggan, *Social Organization of the Western Pueblos* (1950, reissued 1973); Charles H. Lange, *Cochití: A New Mexico Pueblo, Past and Present* (1960, reissued 1990); Alfonso Ortiz, *The Tewa World* (1969); Edward P. Dozier, *The Pueblo Indians of North America* (1970, reissued 1983); Joe S. Sando, *Pueblo Nations: Eight Centuries of Pueblo Indian History* (1992); Bill Wright, *The Tiguas: Pueblo Indians of Texas* (1993); Dorothea C. Leighton and John Adair, *People of the Middle Place: A Study of the Zuni Indians* (1966); C. Gregory Crampton, *The Zunis of Cibola* (1977); T.J. Ferguson et al., *A Zuni Atlas*

(1985); Laura Thompson and Alice Joseph, *The Hopi Way* (1944, reissued 1965); and John D. Loftin, *Religion and Hopi Life in the Twentieth Century* (1991).

Studies of the Apachean tribes include Clyde Kluckhohn and Dorothea Leighton, *The Navaho*, rev. ed., ed. by Lucy H. Wales and Richard Kluckhohn (1962, reissued 1974); Peter Iverson, *The Navajo Nation* (1981); James M. Goodman and Mary E. Goodman, *The Navajo Atlas: Environments, Resources, People, and History of the Diné Bikeyah* (1982); Garrick Bailey and Roberta Glenn Bailey, *A History of the Navajos: The Reservation Years* (1986), an economic and cultural history; Raymond Friday Locke, *The Book of the Navajo*, 5th ed. (1992), a nontraditional, sociocultural history; Morris Edward Opler, *An Apache Life-Way: The Economic, Social, and Religious Institutions of the Chiricahua Indians* (1941, reissued 1965); Donald E. Worcester, *The Apaches: Eagles of the Southwest* (1979); James L. Haley, *Apaches: A History and Culture Portrait* (1981); Richard J. Perry, *Western Apache Heritage: People of the Mountain Corridor* (1991); and Keith H. Basso, *Wisdom Sits in Places: Landscape and Language Among the Western Apache* (1996).

INDEX

A

agglutination, 44
antelope, 4, 8, 47, 53, 73
Apacheans, 81, 88, 90, 93
    Apache, 60, 62, 77, 84, 86, 89,
        90, 91, 99, 109, 110–111,
        112–116
    Navajo, 50, 77, 80, 84–85, 90,
        91, 93, 108, 109, 110, 111–112,
        113, 114, 116–118
Athabaskan languages, 19, 26, 76,
    77–78, 109–110

B

Bannock War, 68
basketwork, 14, 16, 19, 22, 23, 26,
    31, 32–33, 35, 40, 47, 49, 65,
    73, 106, 109, 111
Blessingway, 85
buffalo and bison, 45, 46, 49, 58,
    62, 64, 72, 105, 113

C

Cahuilla, 19–21, 24
California Indians, 95, 97, 119
    food sources and strategies,
        7–8
    history, 1, 14–18
    languages, 16
    matrimony and family, 3, 7,
        12–13
    oral tradition, 9, 13
    religion, 3, 6, 8–11
    shelter, 4
    territorial and political
        organization, 3–4, 6–7
    trade and property ownership,
        3, 5–6
    tribe profiles, 19–41
    visual arts, 3, 13–14
canoes, 8, 21, 40
Carson, Kit, 62, 90, 117
chiefs, 4, 6–7, 13, 23, 26, 29, 30, 31,
    32, 34, 36, 64–65, 66, 98, 113,
    115–116
Christianity, 14, 15, 24, 55, 56, 58,
    86, 88, 89, 105
Chumash, 8, 13, 21–22, 24
Cochise, 75, 112, 116–117
Cocopa, 76, 94
code talkers, 118
Colorado River, 1, 4, 9, 74, 77, 78,
    90, 94, 96, 97, 109, 118
Comanche, 45, 60–65, 69, 72, 112
Costanoans, 22–23, 24
costuming, 9, 14, 31
counting coup, 69
cradleboards, 80

D

dentalium, 26, 28, 35, 40
Diegueños, 9, 23–25
dugouts, 8

E

encomienda, 87, 88

G

Gabrielino, 24, 25–26
Geronimo, 90, 112, 114, 116
Ghost Dance, 57–58
gold rush, 15, 36
Great Basin Indians, 42–43, 119
  food sources and strategies,
    47–49
  history, 55–59
  language, 43, 44–45, 60
  matrimony and family, 51–52
  religion, 43, 52–55, 56, 57–58
  shelter, 46
  social organization, 50
  tools, 47–48
  transportation, 45–46, 50
  tribe profiles, 60–73
  visual arts, 49

H

hogans, 111
Hokan languages, 21, 32, 34, 36,
    44, 45, 60, 76, 95
Hopi, 77, 80, 83, 91, 98, 101, 103,
    105, 106–108, 109, 116
horses, 45–46, 47, 49, 50, 61, 62,
    72, 89, 112, 119
Hupa, 19, 26–28

J

jimsonweed cult, 9, 25, 29

K

kachinas, 82, 83, 84, 88, 107,
    108, 109
Karok, 34
Kawaiisu, 60
Kuksu religion, 8, 9, 14, 30, 31,
    33, 36

L

levirate, 51
Lewis and Clark Expedition, 69,
    70, 71
"Long Walk," 90
Luiseño, 9, 23, 24, 28–29

M

magic, 11, 28, 41, 80, 82
Maidu, 9, 19, 29–30
Maricopa, 76, 94
medicine men and women, 29,
    38, 64, 73
Mission Indians, overview of, 24
missions, 14, 15, 21, 22–23, 24, 28,
    86, 88, 91, 97, 114
Miwok, 30–31
Mogollon, 75, 76
Mojave, 1, 23, 76, 94, 95, 96–97
Mono, 45
  California, 31–32, 65
  Great Basin, 31, 60, 65–66
myths, 9, 52, 85

N

Navajo, 50, 77, 80, 84–85, 90, 91,
    93, 108, 109, 110, 111–112, 113,
    114, 116–118

Northern Paiute, 4, 31, 45, 46, 49, 50, 53, 56, 57, 60, 65, 66–68, 72
Numic languages, 44, 45, 55, 60, 98

O

obsidian, 5, 6, 9

P

Panamint, 45, 60
Parker, Quanah, 63–65
Penutian languages, 19, 22, 29, 30, 35, 76, 77, 108
peyote, 58, 65
Pima, 75, 77, 82, 83, 93–95, 98–99
piñon, 4, 8, 19, 48, 50, 56, 65, 74
polyandry, 51
polygamy, 65
polygyny, 51
polysynthesis, 44
Pomo, 6, 9, 13, 19, 32–33, 35, 38
pottery, 14, 19, 23, 47, 92, 107, 109, 111, 117
Pueblo, 75, 77, 81, 82–84, 86, 87–88, 100–109, 113, 116–117
Pueblo architecture, 79

Q

Quechan, 1, 76, 94, 95, 97

R

ramadas, 111
ritualists, 7, 8, 13
rock painting, 14, 49
Russian colonization, 14

S

Sacagawea, 69, 70–72
salmon, 23, 26, 29, 34, 37, 39, 40, 49, 119
Saubel, Katherine Siva, 20
Serra, Junípero, 14, 15
Serrano, 33–34
shamans, 7, 8, 13, 26, 28, 29, 35, 38, 41, 53, 54, 73, 83, 84
Shasta, 34–35
shells (as currency), 6, 22, 26, 28, 32, 38, 40, 49
Shoshone, 45, 46, 47, 49, 50, 53, 56, 58, 59, 60, 68–72
Sierra Nevada mountains, 1, 29, 30, 31, 74
Snake Dance, 107–108
Sonoran Catholicism, 89
sororate, 51
soul loss, 11
Southern Paiute, 45, 47, 49, 50, 53, 59, 60, 72–73
Southwest Indians, 1, 74–76, 119
    family, 80–83
    food sources and strategies, 78
    history, 86–92
    language, 76–78, 93, 95, 97–98, 109–110
    religion, 83–86, 87–88, 89
    shelter, 79
    social organization, 78, 89
    tribe profiles, 93–118
Spanish colonization, 14, 15, 21, 22–23, 24, 25, 28, 29, 35, 36, 46, 50, 55, 62, 69, 86–89, 97, 101, 105, 108, 110, 111, 112, 114, 116
Sun Dance, 54, 58
sweat lodges, 4, 26, 34, 35, 40

T

teepees, 46, 49, 62, 69, 111
termination, 59, 91
Tohono O'odham, 75, 77, 82, 86, 89, 91, 93–95, 98, 99–100
Toloache religion, 8, 9
tule rafts, 8

U

U.S. Bureau of Indian Affairs, 16, 17, 114
U.S. Indian Reorganization Act, 58–59
usufruct, 5
Ute, 45, 46, 47, 50, 55, 56, 58, 59, 60, 72
Uto-Aztecan languages, 19, 25, 28, 31, 33, 44, 60, 76, 77, 97–98, 101, 106

V

Victorio, 112, 114
vision quest, 53, 54–55, 86

W

Washoe, 1, 44, 45, 46, 50, 52, 53, 55, 60, 73
white-deerskin dance, 9
wickiups, 34, 46, 111
windbreaks, 46, 95
Winnemucca, Sarah, 67–68
Wintun, 9, 19, 32, 35–36
Wodziwob, 57
World Renewal cycle, 41
Wovoka, 57

Y

Yana, 19, 36–37, 44, 95
Yokutsan languages, 19, 65
Yuki, 9, 19, 37–39
Yumans, 23, 76, 85–86, 91, 93–95, 96
Yurok, 19, 26, 28, 34, 39–41

Z

Zuni, 77, 87, 101, 102, 108–109, 112